ANTHOLOGY OF GERMAN POETRY

ANTHOLOGY OF GERMAN POETRY

Through the 19th Century

*In English Translations with
the German Originals*

SECOND REVISED EDITION

Edited by
ALEXANDER GODE
and
FREDERICK UNGAR

FREDERICK UNGAR PUBLISHING CO.
NEW YORK

THIS VOLUME WAS PREPARED WITH THE
EDITORIAL COLLABORATION OF THE
AMERICAN TRANSLATORS ASSOCIATION

Copyright © 1964, 1972 by
Frederick Ungar Publishing Co., Inc.
Printed in the United States of America
Library of Congress Catalog Card No. 73-163479

ISBN: 0-8044-2242-7 cloth
ISBN: 0-8044-6241-0 paper

FOREWORD

'Indeed every translator
is a prophet to his people!'
—*Goethe*

Much has been said, and justly, about the peculiar difficulties of translating poetry. It has even been claimed that any such attempt is doomed to failure. No one can indeed deny that transposing a poem into another language entails the inevitable sacrifice of at least some of its poetic value. Only for very short spans, and this only because of a happy coincidence between two languages in meaning, meter, mood, and diction – something that never happens over long stretches – is the 'absolute' translation achieved.

But should a full acknowledgment of the perils lying in wait for the translator lead to a resigned conclusion that not even an attempt should be made to translate poetry? Is man in all his pursuits, especially in the arts, so committed to the absolute that nothing less is worthy of his endeavors? Or is not rather the opposite true—that acquiescence in the attainable and not the achievement of the absolute is the law of life, and that perfection is no more than a beacon toward which our efforts are directed?

All this, of course, is self-evident; yet it may be well to say it clearly in rebutting the lofty statements so often uttered by poetry's high priests, that if we cannot have perfection we would rather have nothing at all.

There have been many real achievements in translation of poetry, congenial translations that are works of art in their own right; these have often been the triumphs of poets of the first rank who, through the centuries, have been attracted by the challenge of rendering foreign poetry into their mother tongue. This challenge only sharpens what is usually a spontaneous and irresistible desire to make a treasured poem accessible to the many who would surely appreciate it as much, if only they knew it. Those who have undertaken this task – this magnificently exacting task – deserve well of us. They are indeed 'prophets to their people'.

A few words about the unusual genesis of this anthology: This project, undertaken with the editorial collaboration of the American Translators Association, was launched in the conviction that a substantial amount of unpublished translations from the German must surely exist and that lovers of German poetry might be more than willing to attempt new translations for a collection intended to promote the appreciation of German poetry. Invitations went out to professional translators in the English-speaking world, and to members of the teaching profession, to come forth with their personal treasures, or to make this the occasion to complete a long considered translation, or to nominate a favorite version that was the work of someone else.

The response to this invitation was lively beyond expectations; the active interest evidenced by wide participation was highly gratifying.

The great freedom granted the contributors to this anthology in selecting the individual poems to be translated, with only a minimum of direction by the editors, will explain why this collection is not as well rounded as it might otherwise have been. It seemed important to restrict the contributors' own choices as little as possible so as to insure that they would undertake the translation of only those poems for which they felt genuine affinity.

With very few exceptions only new translations are included in this volume. A substantial number of these poems has never before been published in English translation.

The editors would like to think that this anthology has given an added impetus to translators who for some time have been attracted to German poetry but have hesitated to try their hand at an English version because of the slight chance that their efforts would see the light of day. The present volume, it is hoped, may lead the way to a second anthology to be devoted to German poetry of the twentieth-century.

We now release this 'cooperative anthology' to the public without unwarranted claims, but also without apologies for unavoidable imperfections. Creative translation is an unending endeavor – may the next translator testing his mettle on a poem included here achieve a fuller approximation. And may the reception of this volume prove also that many readers agree with our profound conviction that it was worth the effort of so many and that the effort should go on.

FOREWORD TO THE SECOND EDITION

The second edition of this *Anthology*, made possible by the friendly reception of its predecessor, now includes a number of celebrated German poems that were not available in translation for the first. The editors have also omitted several poems that may present difficulties to readers not fully at home in German; all ballads to be found in *A Treasury of German Ballads*, a companion volume, have also been excluded.

There is another reason for shortening the present volume. It is the editors' hope that a compact paperback edition will make this *Anthology* more accessible to a wider audience, particularly to students, who, it is hoped, will be attracted by this collection of many well-loved German poems.

The new translations added to this edition are the work of Gerd Gillhoff, Randolph Macon College; Charles Issawi, Columbia University; Sheema Z. Buehne, Rutgers, The State University of New Jersey; and Alexander Gode, co-editor of the volume.

The fine translations of Alexander Gode are, sadly, the last ones he will contribute. His death in 1970 put an end to a distinguished career in linguistics. Founder and first president of the American Translators Association, a writer and teacher as well as an active translator, Dr. Gode was an inspiration to all who work in this demanding field. All proceeds from the *Anthology of German Poetry* will go into the Alexander Gode fund of the American Translators' Association.

F.U.

TABLE OF CONTENTS

Der von Kürenberg (ca. 1160)

Ich zôch mir einen Valken   2

Unbekannter Dichter

Du bist mîn   4

Walther von der Vogelweide (ca. 1170-1228)

Owê war sint verswunden   6

Paul Gerhardt (1607-1676)

Geh aus, mein Herz   8

Paul Fleming (1609-1640)

An sich   12

Andreas Gryphius (1616-1664)

Abend   14
Eitelkeit der Welt   16
Menschliches Elende   18
Tränen des Vaterlandes   20
Über die Geburt Christi   22

Christian Hoffmann von Hoffmannswaldau (1617-1679)

Wo sind die Stunden   24
Vergänglichkeit der Schönheit   26

August Adolf von Haugwitz (1645-1706)

An sie umb einen Kuß   28

Christian Friedrich Hunold (1681-1721)

Über die Zeit   30

Johann Christian Günther (1695-1723)

Trostaria   32

Friedrich Gottlieb Klopstock (1724-1803)

Die frühen Gräber   34

Matthias Claudius (1740-1803)

Die Mutter bei der Wiege   36
Phidile   38
Der Tod und das Mädchen   42
Kriegslied   44
Die Sternseherin Lise   46
Abendlied   48

Johann Gottfried Herder (1744-1803)

Ein Traum, ein Traum ist unser Leben   52

Ludwig Christoph Hölty (1748-1776)

Mainacht   54

Leopold Friedrich Günther von Goeckingk (1748-1828)

Als der erste Schnee fiel   56
Nach dem ersten nächtlichen Besuche   58

Johann Wolfgang von Goethe (1749-1832)

Das Veilchen   62
Heidenröslein   64
An den Mond   66
Ach, um deine feuchten Schwingen   70
Nachtgedanken   72
Um Mitternacht   74
Harfenspieler   76
Gesang der Geister über den Wassern   78

Lied der Parzen   82
Natur und Kunst, sie scheinen sich zu fliehen   86
Lynkeus der Türmer   88
Zueignung   90
Urworte, Orphisch   92
Symbolum   96
Sprüche   98

Friedrich von Schiller (1759-1805)

Das Glück   106
Das Ideal und das Leben   112
Nänie   116

Friedrich Hölderlin (1770-1843)

Menschenbeifall   118
Sokrates und Alkibiades   120
Abendphantasie   122
Hyperions Schicksalslied   124
An die Parzen   126
Hälfte des Lebens   128
Der Tod   130

Unbekannter Dichter

Ich hab die Nacht geträumet   132

Clemens Brentano (1778-1842)

Wiegenlied   134
Abendständchen   136
Der Spinnerin Lied   138

Ludwig Uhland (1787-1862)

Des Knaben Berglied   140
Frühlingsglaube   142
Auf den Tod eines Kindes   144

Josef Freiherr von Eichendorff (1788-1857)

Der frohe Wandersmann   146

Der Einsiedler   148
Mondnacht   150
Die Nachtblume   152
Waldgespräch   154
Wünschelrute   156

Wilhelm Müller (1794-1827)

Wanderschaft   158
Der Lindenbaum   160

Heinrich Heine (1797-1856)

Leise zieht durch mein Gemüt   162
Es war ein alter König   164
Ein Fichtenbaum steht einsam   166
Die Wanderratten   168
Die Rose, die Lilie, die Taube, die Sonne   174
Wo?   176
Ich hatte einst ein schönes Vaterland   178

Friedrich Hauff (1802-1827)

Reiters Morgengesang   180

Nikolaus Lenau (1802-1850)

An die Entfernte   182
Auf eine holländische Landschaft   184
Schilflied (V)   186
Die drei Zigeuner   188
Die Drei   190
Bitte   192

Eduard Mörike (1804-1875)

Schön-Rohtraut   194
Der Gärtner   198
Das verlassene Mägdlein   200
Um Mitternacht   202
Verborgenheit   204
Denk es, o Seele   206

Ferdinand Freiligrath (1810-1876)

   O lieb, so lang du lieben kannst   208

Friedrich Hebbel (1813-1863)

   Ich und du   212
   Adams Opfer   214
   Der Baum in der Wüste   216
   Sommerbild   218
   Herbstbild   220

Theodor Storm (1817-1888)

   Die Stadt   222
   Juli   224

Gottfried Keller (1819-1890)

   Siehst du den Stern   226
   Abendlied   228
   In der Stadt   230
   Der Schulgenoß   232

Conrad Ferdinand Meyer (1825-1898)

   Jetzt rede du   234
   Der römische Brunnen   236
   Fülle   238
   Zwei Segel   240
   Der Gesang des Meeres   242
   Chor der Toten   244
   Am Himmelstor   246

Ferdinand von Saar (1833-1906)

   Auf einen alten Schloßpark   248

Martin Greif (1839-1911)

   Vor der Ernte   250

Christian Wagner (1835-1918)

Syringen 252

Eugen Höfling (1808-1880)

O alte Burschenherrlichkeit! 254

Detlev von Liliencron (1844-1909)

Die Musik kommt 256

Index of Titles and Beginnings of German Poems 261

Index of Translators 269

```
∪ — ∪ — ∪ — ∪ ∪ — ∪ —
∪ — ∪ — ∪ — ∪ ∪ — ∪ —
∪ — ∪ — ∪ — ∪ — ∪
— ∪ ∪ — ∪ ∪ — ∪ — ∪
```

Nur einen Sommer gönnt, ihr Gewaltigen!
Und einen Herbst zu reifem Gesange mir,
Daß williger mein Herz, vom süßen
Spiele gesättigt, dann mir sterbe!

Die Seele, der im Leben ihr göttlich Recht
Nicht ward, sie ruht auch drunten im Orkus nicht;
Doch ist mir einst das Heilge, das am
Herzen mir liegt, das Gedicht, gelungen:

Willkommen dann, o Stille der Schattenwelt!
Zufrieden bin ich, wenn auch mein Saitenspiel
Mich nicht hinabgeleitet: einmal
Lebt ich wie Götter, und mehr bedarfs nicht.

A single summer grant me, ye Mighty Ones!,
And time wherein to harvest the ripened song,
That willingly my heart, thus slaked in
Rhythmical sweetness may heed the Summons.

The soul whose godlike due is denied it in
This life, finds no repose in the realm of shades.
Yet once the sacred trust I have at
Heart is accomplished – the poem spoken –

Be welcome then, O quiet land of death.
At peace I rest, albeit my lyre cannot
Go with me down to Orcus. Once I
Lived like the gods, and nought else is needed.

Der von Kürenberg

Ich zôch mir einen valken   mêre danne ein jâr.
Dô ich in gezamete   als ich in wolte hân
Und ich im sîn gevidere   mit golde wol bewant,
Er huop sich ûf vil hôhe   und fluog in anderiu lant.

Sît sach ich den valken   schône fliegen:
Er fuorte an sînem fuoze   sîdîne riemen,
Und was im sîn gevidere   alrôt guldîn.
Got sende si zesammen   die gern geliep wellen sin.

I reared me a falcon   longer than one year.
When I had tamed him   as I had willed him be
And I adorned his plumage   with a golden band,
He rose up most high   and flew to another land.

Since then I saw the falcon   grandly flying.
He wore on his foot   a silken ribbon.
The feathers of his wings   were golden fair.
May God bring them together   who fain would be a pair.

Alexander Gode

Unbekannter Dichter

Du bist mîn, ich bin dîn:
Des solt du gewis sîn.
Du bist beslozzen
In minem herzen;
Verlorn ist daz slüzzelîn:
Du muost immer drinne sîn.

I have thee, thou hast me.
Of this thou shalt assured be.
Thou art enlocked
In my heart.
Lost is the key:
Thou must forever in it be.

Alexander Gode

Walther von der Vogelweide

Owê war sint verswunden   alliu mîniu jâr!
ist mir mîn leben getroumet,   oder ist ez wâr?
daz ich ie wânde ez wære,   was daz allez iht?
dar nâch hân ich geslâfen   und enweiz es niht.
nû bin ich erwachet,   und ist mir unbekant
daz mir hie vor was kûndic   als mîn ander hant.
liut unde lant, dar inn ich   von kinde bin erzogen,
die sint mir worden frömde   reht als ez sî gelogen.
die mîne gespilen wâren,   die sint træge unt alt.
unbereitet ist daz velt,   verhouwen ist der walt:
wan daz daz wazzer fliuzet   als ez wilent flôz,
für wâr mîn ungelücke   wânde ich wurde grôz.
mich grüezet maneger trâge,   der mich bekande ê wol.
diu welt ist allenthalben   ungenâden vol.
als ich gedenke an manegen   wünneclîchen tac
die mir sint enpfallen   als in daz mer ein slac,
iemer mêre ouwê.

Alas, whereto have vanished   all my years!
Was, that I lived, but dreaming   or is it true?
All that once seemed so real,   was it so?
I fell asleep thereafter   and now cannot recall.
I have of late awakened,   and all is strange
That in my grasp I fancied   like my other hand.
The people and lands among which   from childhood I grew up
Bear alien looks as though   it was all a lie.
The friends with whom I frolicked   are old and slow.
Our fields lie untended,   our trees long since are felled.
If not the brooks were flowing   as they did of yore,
My haplessness, methinks,   would be complete.
Many greet me vaguely   who once knew me well.
The world is everywhere   burdened with ungrace.
Alas, as I look back   to the glorious days
That are gone as the splurge   of a blow goes from the sea,
Alas, for ever more!

Janet Alison Livermore

Paul Gerhardt

Geh aus, mein Herz, und suche Freud'
In dieser lieben Sommerzeit
An deines Gottes Gaben:
Schau an der schönen Gärten Zier,
Und siehe, wie sie mir und dir
Sich ausgeschmücket haben.

Die Bäume stehen voller Laub,
Das Erdreich decket seinen Staub
Mit einem grünen Kleide:
Narzissus und die Tulipan,
Die ziehen sich viel schöner an
Als Salomonis Seide.

Die Lerche schwingt sich in die Luft,
Das Täublein fleucht aus seiner Kluft
Und macht sich in die Wälder.
Die hochbegabte Nachtigall
Ergetzt und füllt mit ihrem Schall
Berg, Hügel, Tal und Felder.

Die Glucke führt ihr Völklein aus,
Der Storch baut und bewohnt sein Haus,
Das Schwälblein speist die Jungen.
Der schnelle Hirsch, das leichte Reh
Ist froh und kommt aus seiner Höh
Ins tiefe Gras gesprungen.

Go out in this dear summertide
And seek to find the joys that bide
In Heaven's gifts, oh heart:
Behold the gardens' lovely hue,
And see how they for me and you
Are decked by fairest art.

The trees in fullest leafage rise,
The earth, to give its dust disguise,
Has put a green dress on.
Narcissus and the tulip-bloom
Far finer vestment do assume
Than silks of Solomon.

The lark soars high into the air,
The little dove departs its lair
And takes the woodland's way.
The sweetly gifted nightingale
Fills hill and mountain, field and dale
With song, and makes them gay.

The hen leads out her little troop,
The stork does build and fill his stoop,
Its young the swallow feeds.
The hasty stag, the agile doe
Are glad, and from their heights do go
A-running through the reeds.

Die Bächlein rauschen in dem Sand
Und malen sich und ihren Rand
Mit schattenreichen Myrthen.
Die Wiesen liegen hart dabei
Und klingen ganz von Lustgeschrei
Der Schaf' und ihrer Hirten.

Die unverdroßne Bienenschar
Zeucht hin und her, sucht hier und daar
Ihr edle Honigspeise.
Des süßen Weinstocks starker Saft
Kriegt täglich neue Stärk und Kraft
In seinem schwachen Reise.

Der Weizen wächset mit Gewalt,
Darüber jauchzet Jung und Alt
Und rühmt die große Güte
Des, der so überflüssig labt
Und mit so manchem Gut begabt
Das menschliche Gemüte.

Ich selbsten kann und mag nicht ruhn,
Des großen Gottes großes Tun
Erweckt mir alle Sinnen.
Ich singe mit, wenn alles singt,
Und lasse, was dem Höchsten klingt,
Aus meinem Herze rinnen.

The brooklets rustle in the sand
And o'er them and their banks a band
Of shady myrtles keep.
The meadowlands lie close thereby,
Resounding from the happy cry
Of shepherds and their sheep.

The bee-host back and forth has made
Its trips, thus seeking unafraid
Its noble honey-food.
The goodly vine, with juice grown big,
Gets daily in its weakest sprig
Its strength and force renewed.

The wheat grows large with all its might,
And does both young and old delight:
They sing the bounteousness
Of Him Who soothes so generously
And does such countless property
Upon man's spirit press.

Now I can neither rest, nor will:
Great God's great manufactures thrill
Awake my every sense.
I sing along, when all does sing,
And let what shall to Heaven ring
From out my heart commence.

George C. Schoolfield

Paul Fleming

AN SICH

Sei dennoch unverzagt, gib dennoch unverloren,
Weich keinem Glücke nicht, steh höher als der Neid,
Vergnüge dich an dir und achte für kein Leid,
Hat sich gleich wider dich Glück, Ort und Zeit verschworen.

Was dich betrübt und labt, halt alles für erkoren,
Nimm dein Verhängnis an, laß alles unbereut,
Tu, was getan muß sein, und eh man dirs gebeut.
Was du noch hoffen kannst, das wird noch stets geboren.

Was klagt, was lobt man doch? Sein Unglück und sein Glücke
Ist ihm ein jeder selbst. Schau alle Sachen an.
Dies alles ist in dir, laß deinen eiteln Wahn,

Und eh du förder gehst, so geh in dich zurücke.
Wer sein selbst Meister ist und sich beherrschen kann,
Dem ist die weite Welt und alles untertan.

TO HIMSELF

Yet do not be afraid, yet give no post forlorn,
Rise over jealousy, and to each joy assent,
Think it no ill but stay with your own self content,
If fortune, place, and time 'gainst you a league have sworn.

Assume that all has plan, if it do sooth or scorn,
Accept your fate and leave each deed without repent,
What must be done, that do, ere orders speed event.
Whate'er you still can hope, can each day still be born.

Why do men mourn or praise? His fortune, weal or woe,
Is each man to himself. Into each thing inquire –
All this resides in you. Your vain dreams let expire,

And go into yourself, before you farther go:
Who's master of himself and rules his own desire
Has subject unto him the mighty globe entire.

George C. Schoolfield

Andreas Gryphius

ABEND

Der schnelle Tag ist hin; die Nacht schwingt ihre Fahn
Und führt die Sternen auf. Der Menschen müde Scharen
Verlassen Feld und Werk; wo Tier und Vögel waren,
Traurt itzt die Einsamkeit. Wie ist die Zeit vertan!

Der Port naht mehr und mehr sich zu der Glieder Kahn.
Gleichwie dies Licht verfiel, so wird in wenig Jahren
Ich, du, und was man hat, und was man sieht, hinfahren.
Dies Leben kömmt mir vor als eine Rennebahn.

Laß, höchster Gott, mich doch nicht auf dem Laufplatz gleiten!
Laß mich nicht Ach, nicht Pracht, nicht Lust, nicht Angst verleiten!
Dein ewig, heller Glanz sei vor und neben mir!

Laß, wenn der müde Leib entschläft, die Seele wachen,
Und wenn der letzte Tag wird mit mir Abend machen,
So reiß mich aus dem Tal der Finsternis zu dir!

EVENING

The rapid day is gone; her banner swings the night,
And leads the stars aloft. Men's wearied hosts have wended
Away from fields and work; where beast and bird attended,
Now solitude laments. How vain has been time's flight!

The vessel of our limbs draws nearer to the bight.
In but a little while, just as this light descended,
Will I, you, what we have, and what we see be ended.
E'en as a runner's track seems life within my sight.

Great God, grant me that I in coursing do not blunder!
Nor joy trick me nor fear nor woe nor earthly wonder!
Let Your unfailing light my comrade be and guide!

When my tired body sleeps, grant that my soul be waking,
And when the final day my eventide is making,
Then take me from this vale of darkness to Your side!

George C. Schoolfield

EITELKEIT DER WELT

Du siehst, wohin du siehst, nur Eitelkeit auf Erden.
Was dieser heute baut, reißt jener morgen ein;
Wo jetzund Städte stehn, wird eine Wiese sein,
Auf der ein Schäferkind wird spielen mit den Herden.

Was jetzund prächtig blüht, soll bald zertreten werden;
Was jetzt so pocht und trotzt, ist morgen Asch' und Bein;
Nichts ist, das ewig sei, kein Erz, kein Marmorstein.
Jetzt lacht das Glück uns an, bald donnern die Beschwerden.

Der hohen Taten Ruhm muß wie ein Traum vergehn.
Soll denn das Spiel der Zeit der leichte Mensch bestehn?
Ach, was ist alles dies, was wir für köstlich achten,

Als schlechte Nichtigkeit, als Schatten, Staub und Wind,
Als eine Wiesenblum', die man nicht wieder findt!
Noch will, was ewig ist, kein einig Mensch betrachten.

ALL IS VANITY

You see, where'er you look, on earth but vainness' hour.
Tomorrow will destroy that which was built today;
The meadow where the boy a-shepherding will play
Together with his flock, there now the cities tower.

That will be trampled soon which now is full in flower,
The morrow's ash and bone do now defiance inveigh;
No bronze nor marble stands that will not pass away.
Now fortune laughs, but we are soon in hardship's power.

The fame of noble deeds must like a dream desist,
Shall then the toy of time, inconstant man, persist?
Oh, what are all these things for which we long endeavor

But wretched nothingness, but wind and dust and shade,
A flower of the field from which our eyes have strayed!
Yet no man contemplates what will endure for ever.

George C. Schoolfield

MENSCHLICHES ELENDE

(original spelling preserved)

Was sind wir menschen doch! ein wohnhaus grimmer schmertzen,
Ein ball des falschen glücks, ein irrlicht dieser zeit,
Ein schauplatz herber angst, besetzt mit scharffem leid,
Ein bald verschmeltzter schnee und abgebrannte kertzen.

Diss leben fleucht davon wie ein geschwätz und schertzen.
Die vor uns abgelegt des schwachen leibes kleid
Und in das todten-buch der grossen sterbligkeit
Längst eingeschrieben sind, sind uns aus sinn und hertzen.

Gleich wie ein eitel traum leicht aus der acht hinfällt
Und wie ein strom verscheusst, den keine macht auffhält,
So muss auch unser nahm, lob, ehr und ruhm verschwinden.

Was itzund athem holt, muss mit der lufft entfliehn,
Was nach uns kommen wird, wird uns ins grab nachziehn.
Was sag ich? wir vergehn, wie rauch von starcken winden.

HUMAN MISERY

What are we men indeed? Grim torment's habitation,
A toy of fickle luck, wisp in time's wilderness,
A scene of bitter fear and filled with keen distress,
And tapers burned to stubs, snow's quick evaporation.

This life does flee away like jest or conversation;
Those who before us laid aside the body's dress
And in the domesday-book of monster mortalness
Old entry found, have left our mind's and heart's sensation.

Just as an empty dream from notice lightly flees,
And as a stream is lost whose course no might may cease,
So must our honor, fame, our praise and name be ended.

What presently draws breath, must perish with the air,
What after us will come, someday our grave will share.
What do I say? We pass as smoke on strong winds wended.

George C. Schoolfield

TRÄNEN DES VATERLANDES

Wir sind doch nunmehr ganz, ja mehr denn ganz verheeret!
Der frechen Völker Schar, die rasende Posaun,
Das vom Blut fette Schwert, die donnernde Kartaun
Hat aller Schweiß und Fleiß und Vorrat aufgezehret.

Die Türme stehn in Glut, die Kirch ist umgekehret,
Das Rathaus liegt im Graus, die Starken sind zerhaun,
Die Jungfraun sind geschändt, und wo wir hin nur schaun,
Ist Feuer, Pest und Tod, der Herz und Geist durchfähret.

Hier durch die Schanz und Stadt rinnt allzeit frisches Blut.
Dreimal sind schon sechs Jahr, als unser Ströme Flut,
Von Leichen fast verstopft, sich langsam fortgedrungen.

Doch schweig ich noch von dem, was ärger als der Tod,
Was grimmer denn die Pest und Glut und Hungersnot:
Daß auch der Seelenschatz so vielen abgezwungen.

TEARS OF THE FATHERLAND

Entire, more than entire have we been devastated!
The maddened clarion, the bold invaders' horde,
The mortar thunder-voiced, the blood-anointed sword
Have all men's sweat and work and store annihilated.

The towers stand in flames, the church is violated,
The strong are massacred, a ruin our council board,
Our maidens raped, and where my eyes have scarce explored
Fire, pestilence, and death my heart have dominated.

Here through the moat and town runs always new-let blood,
And for three-times-six years our very rivers' flood
With corpses choked has pressed ahead in tedious measure;

I shall not speak of that which is still worse than death,
And crueller than the plague and torch and hunger's breath:
From many has been forced even the spirit's treasure.

George C. Schoolfield

ÜBER DIE GEBURT CHRISTI, 1657

Kind! Dreimal süßes Kind! In was bedrängten Nöten
Bricht dein Geburtstag ein! Der Engel Scharen Macht
Bejauchzet deine Kripp' und singt bei stiller Nacht;
Die Hirten preisen dich mit hellgestimmten Flöten.

Ach um mich klingt der Hall der rasenden Trompeten,
Der rauhe Paukenklang, der Büchsen Donner kracht.
Du schläfst, der tolle Grimm der schnellen Zwietracht wacht
Und dräut mit Stahl und Schwert und Flamm und Haß und Töten.

O Friedefürst! Lach uns aus deinen Windeln an!
Daß mein bestürztes Herz, das nichts als seufzen kann,
Dir auch ein Freudenlied, o Sohn der Jungfrau! bringe.

Doch wenn ich, Gott! durch dich mit Gott in Friede steh,
So kann ich fröhlich sein, ob auch die Welt vergeh,
Indem du in mir ruhst. O Kind! mein Wunsch gelinge!

CONCERNING THE BIRTH OF CHRIST, 1657

Child! Three-times blessed child! In what afflicted ages
Your natal day has dawned! The angel-squadron's might
Your manger celebrates and sings by stilly night,
The shepherd in your praise his bright-voiced flute engages.

Oh, round me rings the cry of trumpets in their rages,
The kettledrum's rough noise, the guns do thunder smite.
You sleep; but yonder wakes swift discord's crazy blight,
And steel and sword and flame and hate and death presages.

Oh prince of peace! To us smile from your swaddling clothes!
That my poor heart, which naught but sighing knows,
May bring you, maiden's son, a song of jubilation.

Yet if I, God, through You may stand in peace,
Then I can still rejoice, although the world may cease,
Since You abide with me. Child, hear my supplication!

George C. Schoolfield

Christian Hoffmann von Hoffmannswaldau

Wo sind die Stunden
Der süßen Zeit,
Da ich zuerst empfunden,
Wie deine Lieblichkeit
Mich dir verbunden?
Sie sind verrauscht. Es bleibet doch dabei,
Daß alle Lust vergänglich sei.

Das reine Scherzen,
So mich ergetzt
Und in dem tiefen Herzen
Sein Merkmal eingesetzt,
Läßt mich in Schmerzen.
Du hast mir mehr als deutlich kundgetan,
Daß Freundlichkeit nicht ankern kann.

Empfangene Küsse,
Ambrierter Saft,
Verbleibt nicht lange süße
Und kommt von aller Kraft;
Verrauschte Flüsse
Erquicken nicht. Was unsern Geist erfreut
Entspringt aus Gegenwärtigkeit.

Ich schwamm in Freude,
Der Liebe Hand
Spann mir ein Kleid von Seide;
Das Blatt hat sich gewandt,
Ich geh im Leide,
Ich wein itzund, daß Lieb und Sonnenschein
Stets voller Angst und Wolken sein.

So sweet, so golden,
Where is the time
When I came first to bolden
And own your beauty's prime
Had me beholden?
It pearled away, as though again to show
That earthly joys which come, must go.

Your plesantnesses,
So arch, so fleet,
Which in my heart's recesses
Found permanent retreat
Have brought distresses.
You more than clearly made me understand
That friendliness is drifting sand.

A kiss's flavor,
Its perfumed taste,
Keeps not for long its savor
And quickly goes to waste.
An emptied quaver
Is little use. For hearts to gather force,
A presentness must be the source.

I swam in pleasure;
The hand of love
Dressed me in silk to measure.
But pain, decreed above,
Fills now my leisure;
And I bewail that love and sunny skies
Prepare for heavy clouds and sighs.

Alexander Gode

VERGÄNGLICHKEIT DER SCHÖNHEIT

Es wird der bleiche Tod mit seiner kalten Hand
Dir endlich mit der Zeit um deine Brüste streichen,
Der liebliche Korall der Lippen wird verbleichen;
Der Schultern warmer Schnee wird werden kalter Sand.

Der Augen süßer Blitz, die Kräfte deiner Hand,
Für welchen solches fällt, die werden zeitlich weichen.
Das Haar, das itzund kann des Goldes Glanz erreichen,
Tilgt endlich Tag and Jahr als ein gemeines Band.

Der wohlgesetzte Fuß, die lieblichen Gebärden,
Die werden teils zu Staub, teils nichts und nichtig werden,
Dann opfert keiner mehr der Gottheit deiner Pracht.

Dies und noch mehr als dies muß endlich untergehen.
Dein Herze kann allein zu aller Zeit bestehen,
Dieweil es die Natur aus Diamant gemacht.

BEAUTY'S TRANSITORINESS

Then pallid death at last will with his icy hand,
Where time hides in the palm, your lovely breasts contain;
The coral of your lips will from its beauty wane,
Your shoulders' warmth of snow will change to icy sand.

Sweet lightning of your eyes, the powers of your hand
That you such conquests make, will but brief hours remain.
Your locks, which presently the glance of gold attain,
The day and year at last will ruin in common band.

Your well-placed foot will then, your movements in their grace,
To naught and nothing part, and part to dust give place.
Before your splendor's god no offering more is laid.

This and still more than this at last must pass away.
Your heart alone has strength its constant self to stay,
Since nature this same heart of diamond has made.

George C. Schoolfield

August Adolf von Haugwitz

AN SIE UMB EINEN KUSS
(*original spelling preserved*)

Der Glantz / der Blitz / die Gluth / die Flammen deiner Augen
Hat mich erschreckt / verblendt / entbrandt und angezündt /
Und einen Durst erweckt / den Hertz und Seel empfindt /
So / dass kein Wasser mehr zum leschen mir wil taugen /

Auch selbst der Thränen nicht so bitter heisse Laugen /
Die doch stets überhäufft aus meinen Augen rinnt /
Und meine Wangen netzt. Drum allerliebstes Kind
Lass mich den Honig-Thau von deinen Lippen saugen /

Der einig ists der mir die heissen Schmertzen kühlt.
Die mein entbrandte Seel' und rauchend Hertze fühlt.
Was seumst du? lesche doch / ach lesche doch geshwind

Den Schmertz / den Durst / den Brandt / das Feuer / diese Hitze /
Den deiner Augen Glantz / und Gluth / und Flamm / und Blitze
Erweckt / ansteckt / gemacht und in mir angezündt.

TO HER FOR A KISS

The shine, the bolt, the glow, the bright flame of your eye
Have frightened, blinded me, enflamed and set alight,
And have awakened thirsts that heart and soul excite,
So that no water can my burning pacify,

Nor e'en the tears themselves, their hot and bitter lye,
Which flows in mighty flood forever from my sight
And irrigates my cheeks. So, child of my delight,
Allow that I your lips of honey-dew suck dry,

For it alone can cool the hot pains of desire,
Which fill my smoking heart, my spirit in its fire.
Why do you hesitate? Drown, drown with all your speed

The pain, the thirst, the flare, the fire-brand, and this heat,
Which your eye's shine and glow and flame and lightning sheet
Awaken, kindle, make, and deep within me breed.

George C. Schoolfield

Christian Friedrich Hunold

ÜBER DIE ZEIT

(*original spelling preserved*)

Ein Pfeil geht zwar geschwind / die Luft saust schnell vorbey /
Die Wolcken lauffen sehr / der Blitz fährt in die Eichen /
Sprich / ob was schnellers noch / als seine Strahlen sey?
Blitz / Pfeil / Lufft / Wolcken sind der Zeit nicht zu
    vergleichen.
Sie streicht geschwind dahin / kein Auge kan es sehn:
Meer / Wind und Wetter sind von Menschen aufzuhalten/
Die Zeit von keinem nicht: sie lässt auch Käyser stehn/
Nicht über einen Blick vermag ein Fürst zu walten.
Wer kauffte nicht die Zeit vor Millionen ein?
Doch geht sie / weil sie mehr als gülden ist zu schätzen. /
Wer sich der Zeit bedient / kan reich in Armuth seyn. /
Bey zeiten kan die Zeit in Glück und Ehren setzen.
Drum edle Menschen braucht anitzt der edlen Zeit;
Gar lange wird der Sand nicht in dem Glase bleiben;
Und sucht die Weissheit mehr als die Ergötzlichkeit /
Vertreibt die Zeit doch nicht / sie wird sich selbst vertreiben.

CONCERNING TIME

An arrow's quick indeed, swift swirls away the air,
The clouds fly on apace, and oak the lightning sears:
Say, whether aught in speed can with its flames compare?
Bolt, arrow, air, and cloud are not the instant's peers.
Time rushes quickly by, no eye its flight intrudes.
Sea, wind, and weather are by men to be delayed,
But time is stopped by none: it emperors eludes,
Not e'en a second can by mighty prince be stayed.
Who would not millions give for time as recompense?
Yet it flies on, since it with more than gold is fraught.
Whoe'er makes use of time has wealth in indigence.
Betimes are men by time to luck and honor brought.
Thus, noble men, do now your noble time employ,
Since sand will not remain for long within the glass;
Seek after wisdom more than you seek after joy,
Make time not pass away: it of itself will pass.

George C. Schoolfield

Johann Christian Günther

TROSTARIA

Endlich bleibt nicht ewig aus,
Endlich wird der Trost erscheinen;
Endlich grünt der Hoffnungsstrauß,
Endlich hört man auf zu weinen,
Endlich bricht der Thränenkrug,
Endlich spricht der Tod: Genug!

Endlich wird aus Wasser Wein,
Endlich kommt die rechte Stunde,
Endlich fällt der Kerker ein,
Endlich heilt die tiefe Wunde.
Endlich macht die Sklaverei
Den gefangnen Joseph frei.

Endlich, endlich kann der Neid,
Endlich auch Herodes sterben;
Endlich Davids Hirtenkleid
Seinen Saum in Purpur färben.
Endlich macht die Zeit den Saul
Zur Verfolgung schwach und faul.

Endlich nimmt der Lebenslauf
Unsres Elends auch ein Ende;
Endlich steht ein Heiland auf,
Der das Joch der Knechtschaft wende;
Endlich machen vierzig Jahr
Die Verheißung zeitig wahr.

Endlich blüht die Aloe,
Endlich trägt der Palmbaum Früchte;
Endlich schwindet Furcht und Weh,
Endlich wird der Schmerz zu nichte;
Endlich sieht man Freudental;
Endlich, Endlich kommt einmal.

CONSOLATION-ARIA

Finally stays no more away,
Finally balm its pledge will keep,
Finally burgeons hope's bouquet,
Finally man will cease to weep,
Finally will the tear-jug break,
Finally death its share forsake.

Finally water turns to wine,
Finally will the right hour peal,
Finally falls the vault's confine,
Finally gaping wounds will heal,
Finally will that slavery
Turn imprisoned Joseph free.

Finally can e'en jealousness,
Finally can e'en Herod end,
Finally David's shepherd-dress
Can its hem to purple lend.
Finally Saul, by time made weak,
Will no more his quarry seek.

Finally will the life-long sum
Of our woes an ending take,
Finally will that savior come
Who our serfdom's yoke can break,
Finally forty years' accrue
Timely makes the promise true.

Finally will the aloe bloom,
Finally will the palm bear fruit,
Finally fear must pass, and gloom,
Finally pain is destitute,
Finally joy's demesne we see,
Finally will some morrow be.

George C. Schoolfield

Friedrich Gottlieb Klopstock

DIE FRÜHEN GRÄBER

Willkommen, o silberner Mond,
Schöner, stiller Gefährt der Nacht!
Du entfliehst? Eile nicht, bleib, Gedankenfreund!
Sehet, er bleibt, das Gewölk wallte nur hin.

Des Maies Erwachen ist nur
Schöner noch wie die Sommernacht,
Wenn ihm Tau, hell wie Licht, aus der Locke träuft,
Und zu dem Hügel herauf rötlich er kömmt.

Ihr Edleren, ach, es bewächst
Eure Male schon ernstes Moos!
O wie war glücklich ich, als ich noch mit euch
Sahe sich röten den Tag, schimmern die Nacht!

THE EARLY GRAVES

Be welcome, O silvery moon,
Silent, beautiful mate of night.
Must you flee? Tarry, remain, philosopher.
See, he remains. 'Twas but clouds wafting along.

There is but the waking of spring
Fairer still than the summer night,
When his curls, shining bright, sprays of dew dispel
And up the hill's sloping side red-hued he comes.

Ye nobler souls, over your stones
Grows already a veil of moss.
Oh how happy I was, when with you I watched
Redness envelop the day, slumber the night.

Alexander Gode

Matthias Claudius

DIE MUTTER BEI DER WIEGE

Schlaf, süßer Knabe, süß und mild!
Du deines Vaters Ebenbild!
Das bist du; zwar dein Vater spricht,
Du habest seine Nase nicht.

Nur eben itzo war er hier
Und sah dir ins Gesicht
Und sprach: „Viel hat er zwar von mir,
Doch meine Nase nicht."

Mich dünkt es selbst, sie ist zu klein,
Doch muß es seine Nase sein;
Denn wenn's nicht seine Nase wär',
Wo hätt'st du denn die Nase her?

Schlaf, Knabe, was dein Vater spricht,
Spricht er wohl nur im Scherz;
Hab' immer seine Nase nicht
Und habe nur sein Herz!

THE MOTHER BY THE CRADLE

Sleep, darling boy, so sweet and mild!
The image of your father, child,
That's what you are; though he insist
That in your face his nose was missed.

And here just now he chanced to be,
And looked into your face,
And said: "He has a lot of me,
But of my nose, no trace".

It is too small, it seems to me,
And yet his nose 'tis sure to be;
For if this proves to be untrue,
How did it come to be with you?

Sleep, son, the things your father says
Are said in jesting part;
You need not ever have his nose,
But only have his heart!

                                        D. G. Wright

PHIDILE

Ich war erst sechzehn Sommer alt,
Unschuldig und nichts weiter,
Und kannte nichts als unsern Wald,
Als Blumen, Gras und Kräuter.

Da kam ein fremder Jüngling her;
Ich hatt' ihn nicht verschrieben,
Und wußte nicht, wohin noch her;
Der kam und sprach von Lieben.

Er hatte schönes langes Haar
Um seinen Nacken wehen;
Und einen Nacken, als der war,
Hab' ich noch nie gesehen.

Sein Auge, himmelblau und klar!
Schien freundlich was zu flehen;
So blau und freundlich, als das war,
Hab' ich noch keins gesehen.

Und sein Gesicht, wie Milch und Blut!
Ich hab's nie so gesehen;
Auch, was er sagte, war sehr gut,
Nur konnt' ich's nicht verstehen.

Er ging mir allenthalben nach
Und drückte mir die Hände,
Und sagte immer O und Ach
Und küßte sie behende.

Ich sah ihn einmal freundlich an
Und fragte, was er meinte;

PHIDILE

I was but sixteen summers old,
All innocence, all wonder . . .
I knew our pasture, knew our world,
But knew of nothing yonder.

Then, from afar, there came a lad.
It was not I who spelled him.
Whatever goal his journey had,
He stayed and said love held him.

He had long lovely silken hair
About his neck a-blowing.
And such a neck! – I've seen not e'er
A neck like that a-growing.

His eyes seemed bluer than the skies
And full of kind endeavor.
Such blue and kind and begging eyes
I had not seen, not ever.

Oh, and his face! Blood-red, milk-white!
I'd seen none such, not ever!
And all he said was true, was right!
For me, though, 't was too clever.

He followed me where'er I went
And took my hands and pressed them
And seemed with Ah's and Oh's all spent
And kissed my hands and blessed them.

Then once, not meaning any harm,
I asked why he was sighing,

Da fiel der junge schöne Mann
Mir um den Hals, und weinte.

Das hatte niemand noch getan;
Doch war's mir nicht zuwider,
Und meine beiden Augen sahn
In meinen Busen nieder.

Ich sagt' ihm nicht ein einzig Wort,
Als ob ich's übel nähme,
Kein einzigs, und – er flohe fort;
Wenn er doch wieder käme!

Whereat my fair lad put his arm
Around me and – was crying.

Such like no one had ever done,
And yet, I did not mind it.
My eyes looked for a place to run
But somehow could not find it.

No single word in what I said
Could mean I was offended.
Not one! But up my lad and fled.
Would he came back! God lend it!

Alexander Gode

DER TOD UND DAS MÄDCHEN

Das Mädchen:

Vorüber! Ach vorüber!
Geh, wilder Knochenmann!
Ich bin noch jung, geh, Lieber!
Und rühre mich nicht an.

Der Tod:

Gib deine Hand, du schön und zart Gebild!
Bin Freund und komme nicht zu strafen.
Sei gutes Muts! ich bin nicht wild,
Sollst sanft in meinen Armen schlafen!"

DEATH AND THE MAIDEN

The maiden:
Pass by me, go, and hie thee
oh, fearsome skeleton!
I am still young! Pass by me,
dear, touch me not, pass on!

Death:
Give me your hand, you lovely, tender maid!
As friend I come, to punish never.
Fearsome I'm not! Be unafraid!
Sleep softly in my arms forever!

Dorothea M. Singer

KRIEGSLIED

'S ist Krieg! 's ist Krieg! O Gottes Engel wehre
Und rede Du darein!
'S ist leider Krieg – und ich begehre
Nicht schuld daran zu sein!

Was sollt ich machen, wenn im Schlaf mit Grämen
Und blutig, bleich und blaß
Die Geister der Erschlagnen zu mir kämen
Und vor mir weinten, was?

Wenn wackre Männer, die sich Ehre suchten,
Verstümmelt und halb tot
Im Staub sich vor mir wälzten und mir fluchten
In ihrer Todesnot?

Wenn tausend, tausend Väter, Mütter, Bräute,
So glücklich vor dem Krieg,
Nun alle elend, alle arme Leute,
Wehklagten über mich?

Wenn Hunger, böse Seuch und ihre Nöten
Freund, Freund und Feind ins Grab
Versammleten und mir zu Ehren krähten
Von einer Leich herab?

Was hülf mir Kron und Land und Gold und Ehre?
Die könnten mich nicht freun!
S' ist leider Krieg – und ich begehre
Nicht schuld daran zu sein!

A SONG OF WAR

The world's at war! O powers above, conspire
To quench the hideous flame!
Alas the war! And I may but desire
That mine be not the blame.

What should I do, if in my dreams the slaughtered
Pale rising should appear,
Bloody accusing ghosts, and silent watered
My bed with many a tear?

If good men, whom my cruel will coerces,
Maimed, wounded unto death,
Should writhe before me in the mire, with curses
Upon their dying breath?

If all these thousands, children, fathers, mothers,
Once happy, sheltered, fed,
Now wretched all, poor people, for those others
Cried woe upon my head?

If want and horror, pestilence, starvation,
Once their dread work were done,
Should gather friend and foe in execration
Of me, the guilty one?

What worth all power to which I might aspire,
The glory and acclaim?
Alas the war! And I may but desire
That mine be not the blame.

Albert Bloch

DIE STERNSEHERIN LISE

Ich sehe oft um Mitternacht,
Wenn ich mein Werk getan
Und niemand mehr im Hause wacht,
Die Stern am Himmel an.

Sie gehn da, hin und her zerstreut,
Als Lämmer auf der Flur,
In Rudeln auch und aufgereiht
Wie Perlen an der Schnur.

Und funkeln alle weit und breit
Und funkeln rein und schön;
Ich seh die große Herrlichkeit
Und kann mich satt nicht sehn. . .

Dann saget unterm Himmelszelt
Mein Herz mir in der Brust:
,,Es gibt was Bessers in der Welt
Als all ihr Schmerz und Lust.‘‘

Ich werf mich auf mein Lager hin
Und liege lange wach
Und suche es in meinem Sinn;
Und sehne mich darnach.

THE STARGAZING MAIDEN

At midnight, after everyone
Has gone to sleep, then I
So often, when my work is done,
Gaze at the stars on high.

They move at random to and fro
Like young lambs pasturing;
They pass in flocks or in a row,
Like peals strung on a string.

And far and wide all twinkle bright
And twinkle pure and still.
I see the splendor of that sight
And cannot get my fill.

Then under heaven's vault my heart
Within me tells me plain,
"The world has something to impart
Beyond its joy and pain."

I throw myself upon my bed
And long I toss and turn,
And ponder what my heart has said,
And lie awake and yearn.

Sheema Z. Buehne

ABENDLIED

Der Mond ist aufgegangen,
Die goldnen Sternlein prangen
  Am Himmel hell und klar;
Der Wald steht schwarz und schweiget,
Und aus den Wiesen steiget
  Der weiße Nebel wunderbar.

Wie ist die Welt so stille
Und in der Dämmrung Hülle
  So traulich und so hold!
Als eine stille Kammer,
Wo ihr des Tages Jammer
  Verschlafen und vergessen sollt.

Seht ihr den Mond dort stehen?
Er ist nur halb zu sehen
  Und ist doch rund und schön!
So sind wohl manche Sachen,
Die wir getrost belachen,
  Weil unsre Augen sie nicht sehn.

Wir stolzen Menschenkinder
Sind eitel arme Sünder
  Und wissen gar nicht viel;
Wir spinnen Luftgespinste
Und suchen viele Künste
  Und kommen weiter von dem Ziel.

EVENING SONG

The silver moon has risen.
The starry heavens glisten
  In golden splendor clear.
The woods stand mute and dreary,
And from the pastures weary
  White fogs surge up afar and near.

The world looks calm and rested,
In twilight shadows vested
  So friendly and so warm.
Just like a quiet shelter
Where you forget the welter
  Of life's distress and every storm.

The moon seems to be growing,
With half of it just showing,
  Yet it is round and fair.
'Tis once again a matter
Of which we blithely chatter
  Though it is not for us to bare.

Prideful, yet mere beginners,
Poor souls we are and sinners,
  We error-stricken souls.
We dream of building towers,
Seek ever greater powers
  And yet stray farther from our goal.

Gott, laß dein Heil uns schauen,
Auf nichts Vergänglichs trauen,
    Nicht Eitelkeit uns freun!
Laß uns einfältig werden
Und vor dir hier auf Erden
    Wie Kinder fromm und fröhlich sein!

Wollst endlich sonder Grämen
Aus dieser Welt uns nehmen
    Durch einen sanften Tod!
Und wenn du uns genommen,
Laß uns in Himmel kommen,
    Du, unser Herr und unser Gott!

So legt euch denn, ihr Brüder,
In Gottes Namen nieder!
    Kalt ist der Abendhauch.
Verschon uns, Gott, mit Strafen
Und laß uns ruhig schlafen
    Und unsern kranken Nachbar auch!

Lord, let us see salvation,
Distrust our passing station
　　And earthly revelry.
Teach us the joys of meekness,
Of strength—beyond man's weakness—
　　In childlike trust and piety.

And when the time is ready,
Grant that, serene and steady,
　　We heed death's gentle nod.
And let us—simple mortals—
Pass through the pearly portals,
　　You, our Lord and our God.

Go, brethren, to—God willing—
Your daily round fulfilling,
　　To rest, each in his room.
Save us, God, from disaster,
Bless our sleep, O Master,
　　And our ailing neighbor's, too.

Alexander Gode

Johann Gottfried Herder

Ein Traum, ein Traum ist unser Leben
Auf Erden hier.

Wie Schatten auf den Wogen schweben
Und schwinden wir,

Und messen unsre trägen Tritte
Nach Raum und Zeit;

Und sind (und wissens nicht) in Mitte
Der Ewigkeit.

A dream – 't is but a dream, our being
Here on this star.

On rolling waves a shadow fleeing
Is all we are.

By clock and rod we gauge our paces
And do not see

Staring at us – before our faces –
Eternity.

Alexander Gode

Ludwig Christoph Hölty

MAINACHT

Wenn der silberne Mond durch die Gesträuche blickt
Und sein schlummerndes Licht über den Rasen geußt
Und die Nachtigall flötet,
Wandl' ich traurig von Busch zu Busch.

Überhüllet von Laub, girret ein Taubenpaar
Sein Entzücken mir vor; aber ich wende mich;
Suche dunklere Schatten,
Und die einsame Träne rinnt.

Wann, o lächelndes Bild, welches wie Morgenrot
Durch die Seel mir strahlt, find' ich auf Erden dich?
Und die einsame Träne
Bebt mir heißer die Wang' herab!

NIGHT IN MAY

Now the silvery moon peeps through the arch of leaves,
Spilling its drowsy light over the walks and lawns,
And the nightingales carol.
Sad, I wander from bush to bush.

Hidden among the leaves, a turtledove and his mate
Coo their rapturous love, making me turn aside,
Seeking gloomier shadows.
And a desolate teardrop falls.

O, you sweet, smiling face, kindling within my heart
All the glory of dawn! Are you only a dream?
And the desolate teardrops,
Brimming over, roll down my cheek.

Helen Sebba

Leopold Friedrich Günther von Goeckingk

ALS DER ERSTE SCHNEE FIEL

Gleich einem König, der in seine Staaten
Zurück als Sieger kehrt, empfängt ein Jubel dich!
Der Knabe balgt um deine Flocken sich
Wie bei der Krönung um Dukaten.

Selbst mir, obschon ein Mädchen und der Rute
Lang nicht mehr untertan, bist du ein lieber Gast;
Denn siehst du nicht, seit du die Erde hast
So weich belegt, wie ich mich spute,

Zu fahren, ohne Segel, ohne Räder,
Auf einer Muschel hin durch deinen weißen Flor,
So sanft und doch so leicht, so schnell, wie vor
Dem Westwind eine Flaumenfeder.

Aus allen Fenstern und aus allen Türen
Sieht mir der bleiche Neid aus hohlen Augen nach;
Selbst die Matrone wird ein leises Ach
Und einen Wunsch um mich verlieren.

Denn der, um den wir Mädchen oft uns stritten,
Wird hinter mir, so schlank wie eine Tanne, stehn
Und sonst auf nichts mit seinen Augen sehn
Als auf das Mädchen in dem Schlitten.

AS THE FIRST SNOW FELL

Like to a monarch who in triumph takes
His way home through his lands, you hear our cheers resound!
And, as for ducats when a king is crowned,
The children battle for your flakes.

Although a maid and from the switch's sway
Long since released, e'en I think you a welcome guest;
Do you not see, since softly you have dressed
The ground, how I no more delay?

Set on a shell, with neither wheels nor sail,
I shall be borne across your meadowland of white
As easily and yet as swift and light
As down before the western gale.

From every window and from every gate
Pale envy will pursue me with her sunken eye;
Seeing me, even the matron lets a cry
Escape, and makes a wish its mate.

For he, who's often been our maiden prey,
Will stand behind me there, as slender as the spruce,
And watching naught else, his eye will not turn loose
The girl before him on the sleigh.

George C. Schoolfield

NACH DEM ERSTEN NÄCHTLICHEN BESUCHE

Bin ich nüchtern, bin ich trunken?
Wach ich oder träum ich nur?
Bin ich aus der Welt gesunken?
Bin ich anderer Natur?
Fühlt' ein Mädchen schon so was?
Wie begreif ich alles das?

Weiß ich, daß die Rosen blühen?
Hör ich jene Raben schrein?
Fühl ich, wie die Wangen glühen?
Schmeck ich einen Tropfen Wein?
Seh ich dieses Morgenrot? –
Tot sind alle Sinnen, tot!

Alle seid ihr denn gestillet?
Alle? Habet alle Dank!
Könnt ich so in mich gehüllet,
Ohne Speis und ohne Trank,
Nur so sitzen Tag für Tag
Bis zum letzten Herzensschlag.

In die Nacht der Freude fliehet
Meine Seele wieder hin!
Hört und schmeckt und fühlt und siehet
Mit dem feinen innren Sinn;
O Gedächtnis! schon in dir
Liegt ein ganzer Himmel mir.

Worte, wie sie abgerissen
Kaum ein Seufzer von ihm stieß,
Hör ich wieder, fühl ihn küssen:

AFTER THE FIRST NOCTURNAL VISIT

Am I sober now or drunk?
Do I wake or only dream?
Have I from creation sunk?
Am I other than I seem?
Suit such feelings maidenhood?
How can they be understood?

Do I know the blooming rose?
Do I hear the raven's cry?
Do I feel how my cheek glows?
Does at wine my taste go dry?
Do I see the dawn turn red?
Dead are all my senses, dead.

Have you all been satisfied?
Take my thanks, if thus you think!
Could I but within me bide
Without food and without drink,
Sit day in, day out apart
'Til the last beat of my heart.

To the night of pleasure flees
Once again my spirit hence,
Hears and tastes and feels and sees
With its keen and inner sense;
Even in you, memory,
Lies a heaven all for me.

All those stuttered words that miss
Meaning, I hear him repeat,
Scarce sighed out – I feel his kiss:

Welche Sprache sagt, wie süß?
Seh ein Tränchen – komm herab!
Meine Lippe küßt dich ab!

Wie ich noch so vor ihm stehe,
Immer spreche: gute Nacht!
Bald ihn stockend wieder flehe:
Bleibe, bis der Hahn erwacht!
Wie mein Fuß bei jedem Schritt
Wanket, und mein Liebster mit.

Wie ich nun, an seine Seite
Festgeklammert, küssend ihn
Durch den Garten hin begleite,
Bald uns halten, bald uns ziehn!
Wie da Mond und Sterne stehn,
Unserm Abschied zuzusehn.

Ach, da sind wir an der Türe!
Bebend hält er in der Hand
Schon den Schlüssel. – Wart, ich spüre
Jemand gehen, Amarant!
Warte nur das bißchen doch!
Einen Kuß zum Abschied noch!

Ich verliere, ich verliere
Mich in diesem Labyrinth!
Träumt ich je, dass ich erführe,
Was für Freuden Freuden sind?
Wenn die Freude töten kann,
Triffst du nie mich wieder an.

Tongue can never tell how sweet!
There's a teardrop – come, descend!
Lips will bring your fall to end!

Now I hold him at arm's reach,
Whispering: "Good night, good night!"
Now I stop and but beseech
Him to stay 'til cock greets light.
My foot, at every move anew,
Falters, and my lover too.

And I see how at his side –
Stopping now, now passing on,
Kissing him – I am his guide,
Tightly nestled, down the lawn,
While the moon and stars convene,
Gazing at our farewell scene.

Oh, now we are at the gate:
Trembling hands are forced to try
The key within the lock. But wait,
Amarant, someone goes by.
Wait for but a moment more!
Take a last kiss at the door!

In this labyrinth I go,
In this maze-way losing me!
Did I dream that I should know
Just how joyful joys can be?
Why, if joy can cause our death,
I have drawn my dying breath.

George C. Schoolfield

Johann Wolfgang Goethe

DAS VEILCHEN

Ein Veilchen auf der Wiese stand,
Gebückt in sich und unbekannt;
Es war ein herzigs Veilchen.
Da kam eine junge Schäferin
Mit leichtem Schritt und munterm Sinn
Daher, daher,
Die Wiese her, und sang.

Ach! denkt das Veilchen, wär' ich nur
Die schönste Blume der Natur,
Ach, nur ein kleines Weilchen,
Bis mich das Liebchen abgepflückt
Und an dem Busen matt gedrückt!
Ach nur, ach nur
Ein Viertelstündchen lang!

Ach! aber ach! das Mädchen kam
Und nicht in acht das Veilchen nahm,
Ertrat das arme Veilchen.
Es sank und starb und freut' sich noch:
Und sterb' ich denn, so sterb' ich doch
Durch sie, durch sie,
Zu ihren Füßen doch.

THE VIOLET

A violet on the lea had grown,
Stood lowly bent and unbeknown;
It was a lovely violet.
Then came a sweet young shepherdess
Of blithesome step and mood to bless
Along, along,
Along the lea and sang.

Ah! thought the violet, could I be
The prettiest flower upon the lea
For just a little while yet,
Until my truelove gathers me
And on her bosom smothers me,
O just, o just
A little moment more.

Alack the day! The maid passed by
And to the violet turned no eye,
Trod on the dainty violet.
It sank and died and still was glad:
Be this the end, the end I've had
Through her, through her,
And at my truelove's feet.

Alexander Gode

HEIDENRÖSLEIN

Sah ein Knab' ein Röslein stehn,
Röslein auf der Heiden,
War so jung und morgenschön,
Lief er schnell, es nah zu sehn,
Sah's mit vielen Freuden.
Röslein, Röslein, Röslein rot,
Röslein auf der Heiden.

Knabe sprach: ,,Ich breche dich,
Röslein auf der Heiden!"
Röslein sprach: ,,Ich steche dich,
Daß du ewig denkst an mich,
Und ich will's nicht leiden."
Röslein, Röslein, Röslein rot,
Röslein auf der Heiden.

Und der wilde Knabe brach
's Röslein auf der Heiden;
Röslein wehrte sich und stach,
Half ihm doch kein Weh und Ach,
Mußt' es eben leiden.
Röslein, Röslein, Röslein rot,
Röslein auf der Heiden.

ROSE AMID THE HEATHER

Saw a lad a rose one day,
Rose amid the heather,
'Twas so fresh and morning-fair
Quick he ran to see it there,
Saw it with much pleasure.
Rose, O rose, O rose so red,
Rose amid the heather.

Said the lad, "I'll pick thee then,
Rose amid the heather!"
Said the rose, "I'll prick thee then,
So thou'lt think of me again,
And I'll bear it never."
Rose, O rose, O rose so red,
Rose amid the heather.

And the wild young laddie picked
Rose amid the heather;
Rose resisted then and pricked,
Crying "Woe!" helped not a bit,
Had to bear it ever.
Rose, O rose, O rose so red,
Rose amid the heather.

Lynda A. Marvin

AN DEN MOND

Füllest wieder Busch und Tal
Still mit Nebelglanz,
Lösest endlich auch einmal
Meine Seele ganz;

Breitest über mein Gefild
Lindernd deinen Blick,
Wie des Freundes Auge mild
Über mein Geschick.

Jeden Nachklang fühlt mein Herz
Froh- und trüber Zeit,
Wandle zwischen Freud und Schmerz
In der Einsamkeit.

Fließe, fließe, lieber Fluß!
Nimmer werd ich froh;
So verrauschte Scherz und Kuß
Und die Treue so.

Ich besaß es doch einmal,
Was so köstlich ist!
Daß man doch zu seiner Qual
Nimmer es vergißt!

TO THE MOON

Filleth glen and dale again
With a hazy sheen,
Setteth free my soul from strain
As it ne'er has been.

Casteth over all I see
Soothingly thy light,
Till the things that have to be
Seem a friendly plight.

Hear, my heart, the old refrain:
Happiness, distress,
Errant between joy and pain
In my loneliness.

Flow, oh flow, dear river, flow.
Happiness has gone.
Banter, kisses vanished so,
And true love anon.

'Twas my own, my very own,
Cherished should it be.
Left of it is pain alone,
Pain of memory.

Rausche, Fluß, das Tal entlang,
Ohne Rast und Ruh,
Rausche, flüstre meinem Sang
Melodien zu!

Wenn du in der Winternacht
Wütend überschwillst
Oder um die Frühlingspracht
Junger Knospen quillst.

Selig, wer sich vor der Welt
Ohne Haß verschließt,
Einen Freund am Busen hält
Und mit dem genießt,

Was, von Menschen nicht gewußt
Oder nicht bedacht,
Durch das Labyrinth der Brust
Wandelt in der Nacht.

Downdale, river, rush along,
Scorn repose and rest.
Rush and whisper to my song
Tunes to meet its quest.

When the storms of winter's night
Make thy banks give way.
When in Spring a surging light
Speeds thy sparkling spray.

Blessed he who, free from hate,
To the world bids leave,
Who in friendship found the gate
Through which to receive.

What, not known to humankind
Or not seen aright,
Through the labyrinthine mind
Travels in the night.

Alexander Gode

Ach, um deine feuchten Schwingen,
West, wie sehr ich dich beneide:
Denn du kannst ihm Kunde bringen,
Was ich in der Trennung leide!

Die Bewegung deiner Flügel
Weckt im Busen stilles Sehnen;
Blumen, Augen, Wald und Hügel
Stehn bei deinem Hauch in Tränen.

Doch dein mildes, sanftes Wehen
Kühlt die wunden Augenlider;
Ach, für Leid müßt' ich vergehen,
Hofft ich nicht zu sehn ihn wieder.

Eile denn zu meinem Lieben,
Spreche sanft zu seinem Herzen;
Doch vermeid, ihn zu betrüben,
Und verbirg ihm meine Schmerzen.

Sag ihm, aber sags bescheiden,
Seine Liebe sei mein Leben;
Freudiges Gefühl von beiden
Wird mir seine Nähe geben.

Ah, your dewy pinions swinging
Eastward, West-wind I would borrow,
For I know that swiftly winging
You can tell him how I sorrow.

Here your swaying wings, oh Blower,
Wake a longing unresisted;
Eye and tree and hill and flower
At your breath in tears are misted.

Yet your wafting, mild and tender,
Cools the eyelids of their burning;
Ah, to grief I should surrender,
But for hope of his returning.

Then to my beloved hasten;
Whisper to his heart; but bidden
To forbear to grieve or chasten,
Wind, my pain from him keep hidden.

Tell, in manner unassuming,
My life is his love unshaken,
And of both a joyous blooming
Will his nearness for me waken.

Aurelia G. Scott

NACHTGEDANKEN

Euch bedaur ich, unglückselige Sterne,
Die ihr schön seid und so herrlich scheinet,
Dem bedrängten Schiffer gerne leuchtet,
Unbelohnt von Göttern und von Menschen:
Denn ihr liebt nicht, kanntet nie die Liebe!
Unaufhaltsam führen ewige Stunden
Eure Reihen durch den weiten Himmel.
Welche Reise habt ihr schon vollendet,
Seit ich weilend in dem Arm der Liebsten
Euer und der Mitternacht vergessen.

NIGHT THOUGHTS

Stars, I pity you and call you hapless!
Ye are beautiful, ye shine in splendor,
Gladly light the way for hard-pressed sailors,
Yet by gods and men are unrewarded:
For ye love not, have of love no knowledge!
Sojournless, eternal hours lead you,
Countless hosts, through infinite expanses.
Think, what journey have ye not accomplished!
While I, ling'ring in my love's embraces,
Thought of neither you nor midnight's passing.

Alexander Gode

UM MITTERNACHT

Um Mitternacht ging ich, nicht eben gerne,
Klein, kleiner Knabe, jenen Kirchhof hin
Zu Vaters Haus, des Pfarrers; Stern am Sterne,
Sie leuchteten doch alle gar zu schön;
Um Mitternacht.

Wenn ich dann ferner, in des Lebens Weite,
Zur Liebsten mußte, mußte, weil sie zog,
Gestirn und Nordschein über mir im Streite,
Ich gehend, kommend Seligkeiten sog;
Um Mitternacht.

Bis dann zuletzt des vollen Mondes Helle
So klar und deutlich mir ins Finstre drang,
Auch der Gedanke willig, sinnig, schnelle
Sich ums Vergangne wie ums Künftige schlang;
Um Mitternacht.

AT MIDNIGHT

At midnight I would walk, somewhat uncertain,
A little lad, along that churchyard site,
To Father's, Parson's, house. The sky's dark curtain
Was strewn so wondrously with starry light,
At midnight.

When later in life's course my dearest love me
Drew to her side, because her spell prevailed—
Contending stars and northern lights above me—
I, going, coming, ecstasies inhaled,
At midnight.

Until at last the full moon's splendor brightly
The inner gloom with clarity replaced,
And thought, responsive, luminous, and sprightly,
The past and future meaningly embraced,
At midnight.

Gerd Gillhoff

HARFENSPIELER

Wer nie sein Brot mit Tränen aß,
Wer nie die kummervollen Nächte
Auf seinem Bette weinend saß,
Der kennt euch nicht, ihr himmlischen Mächte!

Ihr führt ins Leben uns hinein,
Ihr laßt den Armen schuldig werden,
Dann überlaßt ihr ihn der Pein –
Denn alle Schuld rächt sich auf Erden.

SONG OF THE HARP-PLAYER

Who never ate his bread in tears,
Who never sat the night's grim hours,
Weeping, upon his bed in fears,
He knows you not, ye Heavenly Powers!

You lead us into life's broad plain,
Let each live out his guilty birth,
Then give him over to his pain;
For all guilt is avenged on earth.

Herman Salinger

GESANG DER GEISTER ÜBER DEN WASSERN

Des Menschen Seele
Gleicht dem Wasser:
Vom Himmel kommt es,
Zum Himmel steigt es,
Und wieder nieder
Zur Erde muß es,
Ewig wechselnd.

Strömt von der hohen,
Steilen Felswand
Der reine Strahl,
Dann stäubt er lieblich
In Wolkenwellen
Zum glatten Fels,
Und leicht empfangen
Wallt er verschleiernd,
Leisrauschend,
Zur Tiefe nieder.

Ragen Klippen
Dem Sturz entgegen,
Schäumt er unmutig
Stufenweise
Zum Abgrund.

Im flachen Bette
Schleicht er das Wiesental hin,
Und in dem glatten See
Weiden ihr Antlitz
Alle Gestirne.

SONG OF THE SPIRITS OVER THE WATERS

Man's soul
Is like the water:
From heaven descendeth it,
To heaven it riseth,
And down again
To earth it returneth,
Ever repeating.

When rushing headlong
From craggy sheer cliffs
Limpid the current falls,
Vapors rise softly,
Gracefully weaving
Over the barren rock,
Find friendly reception,
Sink, gentle deception,
Murmuring, swirling
Into the depth.

Stones thwart
Its progress,
Brimming ill-humor,
Haltingly floats it
To the abyss.

Caught in the shallows,
Crawls through the valleys;
Unruffled the lake
Mirrors the glory
Of heaven above.

Wind ist der Welle
Lieblicher Buhler;
Wind mischt von Grund aus
Schäumende Wogen.

Seele des Menschen,
Wie gleichst du dem Wasser!
Schicksal des Menschen,
Wie gleichst du dem Wind!

Wind is the lover,
Wave is the bride,
Wind tosses madly
Billows on high.

Soul of man,
Thou art as water,
Fate of man,
Thou art as wind.

R. L. Kahn

LIED DER PARZEN

Es fürchte die Götter
Das Menschengeschlecht!
Sie halten die Herrschaft
In ewigen Händen
Und können sie brauchen,
Wie's ihnen gefällt.

Der fürchte sie doppelt,
Den je sie erheben!
Auf Klippen und Wolken
Sind Stühle bereitet
Um goldene Tische.

Erhebet ein Zwist sich –
So stürzen die Gäste,
Geschmäht und geschändet,
In nächtliche Tiefen,
Und harren vergebens,
Im Finstern gebunden,
Gerechten Gerichtes.

Sie aber, sie bleiben
In ewigen Festen
An goldenen Tischen.
Sie schreiten vom Berge
Zu Bergen hinüber –
Aus Schlünden der Tiefe
Dampft ihnen der Atem
Erstickter Titanen,
Gleich Opfergerüchen,
Ein leichtes Gewölke.

SONG OF THE PARCAE

In fear of the gods let
The race of man stand!
Dominion they hold
In hands everlasting,
With power to use it
As they may see fit.

One whom they exalt
Should fear them twice over.
On cliffs and on clouds
Are chairs set out ready
At tables of gold.

If discord arises,
The guests may be cast,
Abused and dishonored,
To the depths of the dark
And there wait in vain,
Amid gloom and in fetters,
For judgment with justice.

Those others, however,
Sit endlessly feasting
At tables of gold.
And striding from mountain
Across to mountain,
They scent from the chasms
The smoking breath
Of the stifling Titans
Like a thin cloud of odor
Up-wafting from sacrifice.

Es wenden die Herrscher
Ihr segnendes Auge
Von ganzen Geschlechtern
Und meiden, im Enkel
Die ehmals geliebten
Still redenden Züge
Des Ahnherrn zu sehn.

So sangen die Parzen.
Es horcht der Verbannte
In nächtlichen Höhlen,
Der Alte, die Lieder,
Denkt Kinder und Enkel
Und schüttelt das Haupt.

These rulers avert
The eyes of their blessing
From whole generations,
Declining to see
In the grandson the grandsire's
Once well-beloved features
Now mute but eloquent.

So sang the Parcae.
The old one, the exile,
He harkens in hollows
Of night to these songs,
Thinks children and grandchildren,
And shakes his head.

Charles E. Passage

Natur und Kunst, sie scheinen sich zu fliehen
Und haben sich, eh man es denkt, gefunden;
Der Widerwille ist auch mir verschwunden,
Und beide scheinen gleich mich anzuziehen.

Es gilt wohl nur ein redliches Bemühen!
Und wenn wir erst in abgemeßnen Stunden
Mit Geist und Fleiß uns an die Kunst gebunden,
Mag frei Natur im Herzen wieder glühen.

So ists mit aller Bildung auch beschaffen.
Vergebens werden ungebundne Geister
Nach der Vollendung reiner Höhe streben.

Wer Großes will, muß sich zusammenraffen.
In der Beschränkung zeigt sich erst der Meister,
Und das Gesetz nur kann uns Freiheit geben.

Nature, it seems, must always clash with Art,
And yet, before we know it, both are one;
I too have learnt: their enmity is none,
Since each compels me, and in equal part.

Hard, honest work counts most! And once we start
To measure out the hours and never shun
Art's daily labor till our task is done,
Nature once more freely may move the heart.

So too all growth and ripening of the mind:
To the pure heights of ultimate consummation
In vain the unbound spirit seeks to flee.

Who seeks great gain leaves easy gain behind.
None proves a master but by limitation
And only law can give us liberty.

Michael Hamburger

LYNKEUS DER TÜRMER

Zum Sehen geboren,
Zum Schauen bestellt,
Dem Turme geschworen,
Gefällt mir die Welt.
Ich blick in die Ferne,
Ich seh in der Näh
Den Mond und die Sterne,
Den Wald und das Reh.
So seh ich in allen
Die ewige Zier,
Und wie mirs gefallen,
Gefall ich auch mir.
Ihr glücklichen Augen,
Was je ihr gesehn,
Es sei, wie es wolle,
Es war doch so schön!

LYNCEUS THE WARDEN

Conceived to be seeing,
Appointed to sight,
The tower my being,
The world my delight.
I peer in the distance,
I see what is near,
The heavens' persistence,
The fleet-footed deer.
And as I find measure
In all that I view,
I view it with pleasure
And so myself too.
Ye eyes I call blessed,
Of all things ye see
The lasting remembrance
Their beauty will be.

Alexander Gode

ZUEIGNUNG

Ihr naht euch wieder, schwankende Gestalten,
Die früh sich einst dem trüben Blick gezeigt.
Versuch' ich wohl, euch diesmal festzuhalten?
Fühl' ich mein Herz noch jenem Wahn geneigt?
Ihr drängt euch zu! Nun gut, so mögt ihr walten,
Wie ihr aus Dunst und Nebel um mich steigt;
Mein Busen fühlt sich jugendlich erschüttert
Vom Zauberhauch, der euren Zug umwittert.

Ihr bringt mit euch die Bilder froher Tage,
Und manche liebe Schatten steigen auf;
Gleich einer alten, halbverklungnen Sage
Kommt erste Lieb' und Freundschaft mit herauf;
Der Schmerz wird neu, es wiederholt die Klage
Des Lebens labyrinthisch irren Lauf
Und nennt die Guten, die, um schöne Stunden
Vom Glück getäuscht, vor mir hinweggeschwunden.

Sie hören nicht die folgenden Gesänge,
Die Seelen, denen ich die ersten sang;
Zerstoben ist das freundliche Gedränge,
Verklungen, ach! Der erste Widerklang.
Mein Leid ertönt der unbekannten Menge,
Ihr Beifall selbst macht meinem Herzen bang;
Und was sich sonst an meinem Lied erfreuet,
Wenn es noch lebt, irrt in der Welt zerstreuet.

Und mich ergreift ein längst entwöhntes Sehnen
Nach jenem, stillen, ernsten Geisterreich;
Es schwebet nun in unbestimmten Tönen
Mein lispelnd Lied, der Äolsharfe gleich.
Ein Schauer faßt mich, Träne folgt den Tränen;
Das strenge Herz, es fühlt sich mild und weich.
Was ich besitze, seh' ich wie im Weiten,
Und was verschwand, wird mir zu Wirklichkeiten.

DEDICATION*

Again you weave about me, wavering visions,
Who haunted long ago my clouded sight.
Shall I attempt to hold you, apparitions?
Feels still my heart the old illusion's might?
You close and closer surge! Then take dominion,
As you around me rise from mist and night!
The air of magic that surrounds this thronging
Within my breast awakens youthful longing.

Past scenes of joyous days you vivid render,
And with you many cherished shades ascend.
As in an ancient tale, half-muted, tender,
First love, and friendship, too, your train attend.
Grief's felt anew; to mourning it surrenders
O'er life's bewilderingly wayward trend
And o'er the loss of those whom fate has cheated
Of precious hours, their lives ere mine completed.

They cannot hear these lays by me created,
The souls who listened to my earlier songs.
Mute now the warm response that me awaited,
Dispersed forever, oh, the friendly throngs!
My grief by strangers to be heard is fated,
For whose applause my bosom scarcely longs.
The rest, to whom my song once truly mattered,
If still they live, are through the wide world scattered.

A long forgotten yearning now me seizes
For that serene and silent spirit sphere.
Like an Aeolian harp, stirred by faint breezes,
My whispered song falls faltering on the air.
My austere heart its feelings mellows, eases,
A shudder through me thrills, tear follows tear.
All that surrounds me now from sight is banished,
And real becomes what once seemed to have vanished.

Gerd Gillhoff

*Written in the summer of 1797, seven years after the publication of FAUST: EIN FRAGMENT, when the poet had decided to continue work on this drama.

URWORTE, ORPHISCH

Dämon

Wie an dem Tag, der dich der Welt verliehen,
Die Sonne stand zum Gruße der Planeten,
Bist alsobald und fort und fort gediehen
Nach dem Gesetz, wonach du angetreten.
So mußt du sein, dir kannst du nicht entfliehen,
So sagten schon Sibyllen, so Propheten;
Und keine Zeit und keine Macht zerstückelt
Geprägte Form, die lebend sich entwickelt.

Das Zufällige

Die strenge Grenze doch umgeht gefällig
Ein Wandelndes, das mit und um uns wandelt;
Nicht einsam bleibst du, bildest dich gesellig
Und handelst wohl so, wie ein andrer handelt.
Im Leben ists bald hin-, bald widerfällig,
Es ist ein Tand und wird so durchgetandelt.
Schon hat sich still der Jahre Kreis geründet,
Die Lampe harrt der Flamme, die entzündet.

Liebe

Die bleibt nicht aus!—Er stürzt vom Himmel nieder,
Wohin er sich aus alter Öde schwang,
Er schwebt heran auf luftigem Gefieder
Um Stirn und Brust den Frühlingstag entlang,
Scheint jetzt zu fliehn, vom Fliehen kehrt er wieder:
Da wird ein Wohl im Weh, so süß und bang.
Gar manches Herz verschwebt im Allgemeinen,
Doch widmet sich das edelste dem Einen.

PRIMEVAL WORDS, ORPHIC

Daimon

As on the day in which your life began
The sun to stars and planets was related,
So you unfolded, following a plan
Determined on the day you were created.
Thus you must be, escape you never can,
Sibyls and prophets long ago thus stated.
And neither time nor force can ever break
The finished form that growing life will take.

Chance

These strict confines are softly bypassed, though,
By change that changes with us as we stride.
You do not stay alone; with friends you come and go,
You act indeed like others by your side.
Life brings adjustment, motion to and fro—
It is an idle ride, and so you ride.
Soon year and year in rounding chain combine,
The lamp awaits the spar, to make it shine.

Love

And it will come! Down from the sky he flings
Himself, to which from earthly dust he rose.
He floats along upon his airy wings;
Around his head and chest a spring day flows.
He seems to flee, then back from flight he swings,
While bliss from pain, or joy from anguish, grows.
The hearts of many men may hither float, or yon;
The noblest heart, however, stays with one.

Nötigung

Da ists denn wieder, wie die Sterne wollten:
Bedingung und Gesetz, und aller Wille
Ist nur ein Wollen, weil wir eben sollten,
Und vor dem Willen schweigt die Willkür stille;
Das Liebste wird vom Herzen weggescholten,
Dem harten Muß bequemt sich Will und Grille.
So sind wir scheinfrei denn, nach manchen Jahren
Nur enger dran, als wir am Anfang waren.

Hoffnung

Doch solcher Grenze, solcher ehrnen Mauer
Höchst widerwärt'ge Pforte wird entriegelt,
Sie stehe nur mit alter Felsendauer!
Ein Wesen regt sich leicht und ungezügelt:
Aus Wolkendecke, Nebel, Regenschauer
Erhebt sie uns, mit ihr, durch sie beflügelt,
Ihr kennt sie wohl, sie schwärmt durch alle Zonen—
Ein Flügelschlag—und hinter uns Äonen!

Necessity

There 'tis again—the planets' whim, anew:
All regulations, laws, and every will
Are only willed as something we must do.
Where will prevails, caprice must come to nil;
Your heart's desires shall be withheld from you,
And that which Must commands, Will must fulfill.
Thus freedom—an illusion of the heart—
Has, after years, more limits than at start.

Hope

The gate, though, in this wall of limitation,
Shall soon be opened up—that hateful gate!
Let it but stand upon its firm foundation!
A spirit rises from it, free and straight.
She lifts us on her wings to liberation;
From clouds and mist toward a better fate.
Familiar is her flight, and to no land confined;
One stroke of wings—and eons lie behind!

Max Knight and Joseph Fabry

SYMBOLUM

Die Zukunft decket
Schmerzen und Glücke
Schrittweis dem Blicke,
Doch ungeschrecket
Dringen wir vorwärts.

Und schwer und ferne
Hängt eine Hülle
Mit Ehrfurcht. – Stille
Ruhn oben die Sterne
Und unten die Gräber.

Doch rufen von drüben
Die Stimmen der Geister,
Die Stimmen der Meister:
„Versäumt nicht zu üben
Die Kräfte des Guten!

Hier flechten sich Kronen
In ewiger Stille,
Die sollen mit Fülle
Die Tätigen lohnen!
Wir heißen euch hoffen!"

SYMBOLUM

The future holds hidden
Blessings and sorrows
In rows of tomorrows. —
Undaunted, unbidden
We keep pressing forward.

Heavy and far
Of awe a curtain.
Star beyond star
Above. And certain
The graves below.

But voices we hallow
Of masters preceding
Invoke our heeding:
"Let never lie fallow
The forces of good.

We gather forever
In infinite calm
The laurel, the palm
For lives of endeavor —
And bid you have hope."

Alexander Gode

SPRÜCHE

Geheimnisvoll am lichten Tag
Läßt sich Natur des Schleiers nicht berauben,
Und was sie deinem Geist nicht offenbaren mag,
Das zwingst du ihr nicht ab mit Hebeln und mit Schrauben.

Jesus fühlte rein und dachte
Nur den einen Gott im Stillen;
Wer ihn selbst zum Gotte machte,
Kränkte seinen heilgen Willen.

Laß nur die Sorge sein,
Das gibt sich alles schon;
Und fällt der Himmel ein,
Kommt doch eine Lerche davon.

Mann mit zugeknöpften Taschen,
Dir tut niemand was zulieb.
Hand wird nur von Hand gewaschen:
Wenn du nehmen willst, so gib!

Wenn ein kluger Mann der Frau befiehlt,
Dann sei es um ein Großes gespielt;
Will die Frau dem Mann befehlen,
So muß sie das Große im Kleinen wählen.

Welche Frau hat einen guten Mann
Der sieht man's am Gesicht wohl an.

Denn wir können die Kinder nach unserem Sinne nicht formen;
So wie Gott sie uns gab, so muß man sie haben und lieben,
Sie erziehen aufs beste und jeglichen lassen gewähren.

SAYINGS

Mysterious in light of day,
Her veils doth Nature freely loosen never,
And all the secrets she will not to thee display
Thou shalt not worm away from her with prize and lever.

Pure was Jesus in his passion,
In his heart but one God serving;
Who of him a God would fashion
From his sacred will is swerving.

Forsake your worries all –
You have come through many a scrape –
And should the heavens fall,
One lark is sure to escape.

Button not thy pockets, brother,
None will thee a kindness give;
One hand's washed but by another,
Thou must give, wouldst thou receive!

When a shrewd man his wife command,
Let major issues be at hand;
But would a wife command her spouse,
The big within the little she must choose.

By a wife's face it may be known
That a good husband she doth own.

Children can scarcely be fashioned to meet with our likes and our
purpose.
Just as God did us give them, so must we hold them and love
them,
Nurture and teach them to fullness and leave them to be what
they are.

Wer Wissenschaft und Kunst besitzt,
Hat auch Religion.
Wer jene beiden nicht besitzt,
Der habe Religion.

Müsset im Naturbetrachten
Immer eins wie alles achten:
Nichts ist drinnen, nichts ist draußen:
Denn was innen, das ist außen.
So ergreifet ohne Säumnis
Heilig öffentlich Geheimnis.

Wär' nicht das Auge sonnenhaft,
Nie könnte es die Sonn' erblicken
Wär' nicht in uns des Gottes eig'ne Kraft,
Wie könnt' uns Göttliches entzücken?

Was hieße wohl die Natur ergründen? –
Gott ebenso außen wie innen zu finden.

Was wär' ein Gott, der nur von außen stieße,
Im Kreis das All am Finger laufen ließe?
Ihm ziemt's, die Welt im Innern zu bewegen,
Natur in Sich, Sich in Natur zu hegen,
So daß, was in Ihm lebt und webt und ist,
Nie Seine Kraft, nie Seinen Geist vermißt.

Im Atemholen sind zweierlei Gnaden:
Die Luft einziehen, sich ihrer entladen;
Jenes bedrängt, dieses erfrischt;
So wunderbar ist das Leben gemischt.
Du danke Gott, wenn er dich preßt,
Und dank ihm, wenn er dich wieder entläßt.

He has religion
Who has art and science.
Who has not art nor science,
Needs have religion.

Heinz Norden

In your nature observation
One and all want equal station.
Nothing's inside, nothing's outside,
For the inside is the outside.
Grasp without procrastination
Patent-occult revelation.

Were not the eye born of the sun,
The sun could not by it be sighted.
Had our life not in God's strength begun,
How could by things divine we be delighted?

What is it we probers of Nature are seeking? –
Out there the God whom within we hear speaking!

What would a god be who but gave the world
A push to have it spin around His finger?
Him it behooves to move things from within
Comprising Nature and comprised by Her,
So that what in Him grows and flows and is
Must share the strength and spirit that are His.

In taking breath thou hast two kinds of blessing:
The air intracting, the air egressing.
The one feels anxious, the other refreshed.
Thus strangely too is thy life enmeshed.
Thou thank thy God Which presses thee;
And thank him further when He sets thee free.

Freudvoll
Und leidvoll,
Gedankenvoll sein,
Langen
Und bangen
In schwebender Pein,
Himmelhoch jauchzend,
Zum Tode betrübt –
Glücklich allein
Ist die Seele, die liebt.

Das Alter ist ein höflich Mann:
Einmal übers andre klopft er an,
Aber nun sagt niemand: Herein!
Und vor der Türe will er nicht sein.
Da klinkt er auf, tritt ein so schnell,
Und nun heißts, er sei ein grober Gesell.

Nie verläßt uns der Irrtum, doch ziehet ein höher Bedürfnis
Immer den strebenden Geist leise zur Wahrheit hinan.

Wer mit dem Leben spielt,
Kommt nie zurecht;
Wer sich nicht selbst befiehlt,
Bleibt immer ein Knecht.

Vergebens werden ungebundne Geister
nach der Vollendung reiner Höhe streben.
Wer Großes will, muß sich zusammenraffen.
In der Beschränkung zeigt sich erst der Meister,
und das Gesetz nur kann uns Freiheit geben.

Willst du ins Unendliche schreiten,
Geh im Endlichen nach allen Seiten.

Gladdened
And saddened
In thoughtful refrain,
Worried
And sorried
In lingering pain,
Cheered to high heaven,
Depressed to deep gloom,
Happy is fain
But a soul in love's bloom.

Age is a very courteous chap.
Knocks on the door with many a rap.
But bid him in no one does care.
And since he finds it cold out there,
At length he slips in quick and sure.
And now we call him a beastly boor.

Never will error release us, but always transcendent endeavor
Leads on the mind which persists, nearer – most gently – to truth.

Who lives by sleight of hand
Is bound to fall.
Who fails in self-command
Remains a thrall.

It is in vain when talent loath of bridle
Tries to attain the crown of full perfection.
He who aims high must gladly brook the harness:
To prove himself the master needs restriction,
And rule alone can give a man his freedom.

Wilt thou into infinities wander,
Roam through the finite hither and yonder.

Volk und Knecht und Überwinder,
Sie gestehn zu jeder Zeit:
Höchstes Glück der Erdenkinder
Sei nur die Persönlichkeit.
Jedes Leben sei zu führen,
Wenn man sich nicht selbst vermißt;
Alles könne man verlieren,
Wenn man bliebe, was man ist.

Ja! diesem Sinne bin ich ganz ergeben,
Das ist der Weisheit letzter Schluß:
Nur der verdient sich Freiheit wie das Leben,
Der täglich sie erobern muß.

Schaff, das Tagwerk meiner Hände,
Hohes Glück, daß ich's vollende!
Laß, o laß mich nicht ermatten!
Nein, es sind nicht leere Träume:
Jetzt nur Stangen, diese Bäume
Geben einst noch Frucht und Schatten.

Those in bondage, those in power,
All men of all times agree
That no fortune can be greater
Than man's personality,
That no life deserves man's scorning
If he, what he is, remains,
That no loss is worth his mourning
If his self he but retains.

This I believe with passionate obsession
And call it wisdom's ultimate advice:
None keeps of life and liberty possession,
But daily pays in sweat and toil their price.

Give me – bliss of daily striving –
Give me trust it will be thriving!
Keep my strength, keep it from fading!
No, it is not idle dreaming:
Spindly stalks these trees now seeming
Will in time give fruit and shading.

Alexander Gode

Friedrich Schiller

DAS GLÜCK

Selig, welchen die Götter, die gnädigen, vor der Geburt schon
  Liebten, welchen als Kind Venus im Arme gewiegt,
Welchem Phöbus die Augen, die Lippen Hermes gelöset
  Und das Siegel der Macht Zeus auf die Stirne gedrückt!
Ein erhabenes Los, ein göttliches, ist ihm gefallen,
  Schon vor des Kampfes Beginn sind ihm die Schläfen bekränzt.
Ihm ist, eh er es lebte, das volle Leben gerechnet,
  Eh er die Mühe bestand, hat er die Charis erlangt.

Groß zwar nenn' ich den Mann, der, sein eigner Bildner und Schöpfe
  Durch der Tugend Gewalt selber die Parze bezwingt;
Aber nicht erzwingt er das Glück, und was ihm die Charis
  Neidisch geweigert, erringt nimmer der strebende Mut.
Vor Unwürdigem kann dich der Wille, der ernste, bewahren,
  Alles Höchste, es kommt frei von den Göttern herab.
Wie die Geliebte dich liebt, so kommen die himmlischen Gaben;
  Oben in Jupiters Reich herrscht, wie in Amors, die Gunst.
Neigungen haben die Götter, sie lieben der grünenden Jugend
  Lockigte Scheitel, es zieht Freude die Fröhlichen an.
Nicht der Sehende wird von ihrer Erscheinung beseligt,
  Ihrer Herrlichkeit Glanz hat nur der Blinde geschaut.
Gern erwählen sie sich der Einfalt kindliche Seele,
  In das bescheidne Gefäß schließen sie Göttliches ein.
Ungehofft sind sie da und täuschen die stolze Erwartung,
  Keines Bannes Gewalt zwinget die Freien herab.
Wem er geneigt, dem sendet der Vater der Menschen und Götter
  Seinen Adler herab, trägt ihn zu himmlischen Höhn.

THE GIFTS OF FORTUNE

Blessed whom, ere he was born, the gods for their favors had chosen,
    Whom, while he was but a child, Venus held up in her arms.
Phoebus opens his eyes, his lips are untied by Hermes,
    And the emblem of might Zeus imprints on his brow.
Truly, sublime is his prospect. The fate that befell him is godlike.
    His is the victor's crown long ere the fray has begun;
Long ere he starts on his journey, its goal is reckoned
            accomplished;
    Ere he has proven his worth, safe he stands sheltered in grace.

Great, to be sure, will I call the other who – self-made and
            self-trained –
    Alters, by virtue's strength, even the Moira's decree.
Never the gifts of Fortune will thus be compelled. What is given
    Only by grace must remain outside the pale of man's will.
Earnest endeavor can help one to vanquish the powers of evil,
    But the ultimate good unbidden descends from on high.
Heaven bestows its gifts as love is bestowed by lovers:
    Favor rules Cupid's realm, likewise the realm of Zeus.
Think not the gods impartial. The curls of youth may bewitch them.
    Gay in their hearts themselves, fain with the gay they consort.
Not the keen-eyed observer is granted the bliss to behold them;
    Only the unknowing blind witness their splendorous light.
Often they choose for their gifts the simple soul of the childlike,
    Casting in humblest forms substance of heavenly kin.
Coming where least awaited, they foil him who proudly expects them:
    There is no magic, no spell potent to cast them in bonds.
Whom the Father of men and Immortals has chosen his minion
    He bids his eagle seek out, carry to heavenly heights.

Unter die Menge greift er mit Eigenwillen, und welches
    Haupt ihm gefället, um das flicht er mit liebender Hand
Jetzt den Lorbeer und jetzt die herrschaftgebende Binde,
    Krönte doch selber den Gott nur das gewogene Glück.

Vor dem Glücklichen her tritt Phöbus, der pythische Sieger,
    Und, der die Herzen bezwingt, Amor, der lächelnde Gott.
Vor ihm ebnet Poseidon das Meer, sanft gleitet des Schiffes
    Kiel, das den Cäsar führt und sein allmächtiges Glück.
Ihm zu Füßen legt sich der Leu, das brausende Delphin
    Steigt aus den Tiefen, und fromm beut es den Rücken ihm an.

Zürne dem Glücklichen nicht, daß den leichten Sieg ihm die Götter
    Schenken, daß aus der Schlacht Venus den Liebling entrückt.
Ihn, den die Lächelnde rettet, den Göttergeliebten beneid' ich,

    Jenen nicht, dem sie mit Nacht deckt den verdunkelten Blick.
War er weniger herrlich, Achilles, weil ihm Hephästos
    Selbst geschmiedet den Schild und das verderbliche Schwert?
Weil um den sterblichen Mann der große Olymp sich beweget?
    Das verherrlichet ihn, daß ihn die Götter geliebt,
Daß sie sein Zürnen geehrt und, Ruhm dem Liebling zu geben,
    Hellas' bestes Geschlecht stürzten zum Orkus hinab.
Zürne der Schönheit nicht, daß sie schön ist, daß sie verdienstlos,
    Wie der Lilie Kelch prangt durch der Venus Geschenk!
Laß sie die Glückliche sein; du schaust sie, du bist der Beglückte!

    Wie sie ohne Verdienst glänzt, so entzücket sie dich.
Freue dich, daß die Gabe des Lieds vom Himmel herabkommt,
    Daß der Sänger dir singt, was ihn die Muse gelehrt:
Weil der Gott ihn beseelt, so wird er dem Hörer zum Gotte;
    Weil er der Glückliche ist, kannst du der Selige sein.
Auf dem geschäftigen Markt, da führe Themis die Waage,
    Und es messe der Lohn streng an der Mühe sich ab;

Guided by whim or fancy, the god finds the one among many
    Whom he decides to like, and with a loving hand
Crowns with laurels or fillet of power the head he has chosen,
    For, he himself wears his crown only by Fortune's grace.

Smoothed is the path of the fortunate mortal by Phoebus Apollo
    And the subduer of hearts, Amor, the smiling god.
Neptune quiets the ocean before him, and blithely his vessel –
    "Caesar aboard and his luck" – follows his charted course.
Gently the lion lies down at his feet, and the agile dolphin
    Pushes its back into view, ready to serve as his mount.

Do not resent that the gods grant the favored few effortless triumphs
    Or that whom Venus prefers safely she whisks from the fight.
Worthy of praise deems the world whom the smiling goddess has
        rescued,
    Paying the other no heed whom she let sink to the shades.
Do we account Achilles' glory impaired since Hephaestus
    Fashioned his mighty shield and his destructive sword,
Since for this one mortal human all of Olympus is stirring?
    No, it glorifies him that he is loved by the gods,
That they would honor his wrath, and, for the sake of his glory,
    Plunge the flower of Greece into the Hadean night.
Do not resent that beauty's beauty stems from no merit,
    That it is Venus's gift, free as the blossoms of Spring.
Let beauty enjoy its good fortune. Behold it and share the
        enjoyment.
    Undeserved are its charms. So is your power to see.
Let us rejoice that the gift of song has descended from heaven,
    That the poet, for us, sings what he learned from the Muse.
Holding his fief from a god, he appears as a god to us hearers,
    Being by Fortune endowed, bliss he reflects upon us.
In the affairs of the market let Themis hold sway with her balance.
    There the weight of the toil measures by rights the reward.

Aber die Freude ruft nur ein Gott auf sterbliche Wangen,
    Wo kein Wunder geschieht, ist kein Beglückter zu sehn.

Alles Menschliche muß erst werden und wachsen und reifen,
    Und von Gestalt zu Gestalt führt es die bildende Zeit;
Aber das Glückliche siehest du nicht, das Schöne nicht werden,
    Fertig von Ewigkeit her steht es vollendet vor dir.
Jede irdische Venus ersteht, wie die erste des Himmels,
    Eine dunkle Geburt, aus dem unendlichen Meer;
Wie die erste Minerva, so tritt, mit der Ägis gerüstet,
    Aus des Donnerers Haupt jeder Gedanke des Lichts.

Not so with joy. It appears when a god has decreed its appearance:
  Only a miracle can conjure its warmth to men's hearts.

Everything human must slowly arise, must unfold, and must ripen:
  Ever from phase to phase plastic time leads it on.
But neither beauty nor fortune are ever born into being:
  Perfect ere time began, perfect they face us today.
Every Venus on earth emerges, as did the divine one,
  As an occult event from the infinite sea.
Perfect, like the divine Minerva, equipped with the aegis,
  So every light-bearing thought springs from the Thunderer's head.

                                        Alexander Gode

DAS IDEAL UND DAS LEBEN

Ewigklar und spiegelrein und eben
Fließt das zephyrleichte Leben
Im Olymp den Seligen dahin.
Monde wechseln und Geschlechter fliehen,
Ihrer Götterjugend Rosen blühen
Wandellos im ewigen Ruin.
Zwischen Sinnenglück und Seelenfrieden
Bleibt dem Menschen nur die bange Wahl.
Auf der Stirn des hohen Uraniden
Leuchtet ihr vermählter Strahl.

Wollt ihr schon auf Erden Göttern gleichen,
Frei sein in des Todes Reichen,
Brechet nicht von seines Gartens Frucht.
An dem Scheine mag der Blick sich weiden,
Des Genusses wandelbare Freuden
Rächet schleunig der Begierde Flucht.
Selbst der Styx, der neunfach sie umwindet,
Wehrt die Rückkehr Ceres Tochter nicht,
Nach dem Apfel greift sie und es bindet
Ewig sie des Orkus Pflicht.

Nur der Körper eignet jenen Mächten,
Die das dunkle Schicksal flechten,
Aber frei von jeder Zeitgewalt,
Die Gespielin seliger Naturen
Wandelt oben in des Lichtes Fluren,
Göttlich unter Göttern, die Gestalt.
Wollt ihr hoch auf ihren Flügeln schweben,
Werft die Angst des Irdischen von euch,
Fliehet aus dem engen dumpfen Leben
In des Ideales Reich!

THE IDEAL AND LIFE

Tranquil and pure as glass, forever clear,
Soft as a zephyr, unassailed by fear,
For the Olympian gods life gently flows.
The generations pass, moons wax and wane,
Immutable amid eternal bane,
For them, the gods, forever blooms the rose.
In human life a fearful course is run
Between the senses and peace of the soul.
But on the lofty brow of Saturn's son
These two unite to make one radiant whole.

If you would be like gods upon the earth
And wander freely in the realms of Death.
Pluck no morsels of his garden's fruit.
Safe to delight the eye in outward showing,
But perilous to taste what there is growing,
For having punishes desire's pursuit.
Even the Styx, entwined ninefold around her,
Cannot prevent Proserpine's return.
Once she has grasped the apple, it has bound her
To Hades for an everlasting sojourn.

The flesh alone is prey to those dark powers
Ever weaving at our destinies;
Freed of bondage to the hours,
Playmate of blissful entities,
The pure form rises to Elysian bowers,
Itself divine among divinities.
If you would soar as high upon its wings,
Cast off the terrors of mortality,
Flee from the narrowness of daily things
Into the realm of ideality.

Jugendlich, von allen Erdenmalen
Frei, in der Vollendung Strahlen
Schwebet hier der Menschheit Götterbild,
Wie des Lebens schweigende Phantome
Glänzend wandeln an dem stygschen Strome,
Wie sie stand im himmlischen Gefild,
Ehe noch zum traurgen Sarkophage
Die Unsterbliche herunter stieg.
Wenn im Leben noch des Kampfes Waage.
Schwankt, erscheinet hier der Sieg.

.   .   .   .

Wenn das Tote bildend zu beseelen,
Mit dem Stoff sich zu vermählen
Tatenvoll der Genius entbrennt,
Da, da spanne sich des Fleißes Nerve,
Und beharrlich ringend unterwerfe
Der Gedanke sich das Element.
Nur dem Ernst, den keine Mühe bleichet,
Rauscht der Wahrheit tief versteckter Born,
Nur des Meißels schwerem Schlag erweichet
Sich des Marmors sprödes Korn.

Aber dringt bis in der Schönheit Sphäre,
Und im Staube bleibt die Schwere
Mit dem Stoff, den sie beherrscht, zurück.
Nicht der Masse qualvoll abgerungen,
Schlank und leicht, wie aus dem Nichts gesprungen,
Steht das Bild vor dem entzückten Blick.
Alle Zweifel, alle Kämpfe schweigen
In des Sieges hoher Sicherheit,
Ausgestoßen hat es jeden Zeugen
Menschlicher Bedürftigkeit.

There, young and free from any earthly stain,
Soaring in perfect being's high domain,
There is man's image of divinity,
As life's silent phantoms like bright gleams
Drift along beside the Stygian streams,
As, amid the field of heaven, she,
The Immortal, stood before descending
Into the mournful burial vaults below.
When in life the struggle seems unending,
Suddenly we sense sweet victory's glow.

.   .   .   .

When the spirit kindles with desire
To shape dead matter, lend it life's own fire,
To take crude mass and pass it on refined—
It must be done by straining every nerve;
Only unflinching constancy will serve
To subjugate the elements to Mind.
For Truth in her mysterious deep spring
Yields only to the one who spares no pain.
As marble only can be made to sing
Under the chisel's merciless refrain.

But once the shape of beauty has been found
All weight lies with the chips upon the ground.
And from the massive block, now free to rise,
Slender and light, as it were made of air,
Showing no trace of all the pangs and care,
The statue stands before enraptured eyes.
For all the doubts and struggles now have vanished
In the sureness of a victory,
And every single sign has now been banished
That spoke to us of human poverty.

Richard Winston

NÄNIE

Auch das Schöne muß sterben! Das Menschen und Götter bezwinget,
  Nicht die eherne Brust rührt es des stygischen Zeus.
Einmal nur erweichte die Liebe den Schattenbeherrscher,
  Und an derSchwelle noch, streng, rief er zurück sein Geschenk.
Nicht stillt Aphrodite dem schönen Knaben die Wunde,
  Die in den zierlichen Leib grausam der Eber geritzt.
Nicht errettet den göttlichen Held die unsterbliche Mutter,
  Wann er, am skäischen Tor fallend, sein Schicksal erfüllt.
Aber sie steigt aus dem Meer mit allen Töchtern des Nereus,
  Und die Klage hebt an um den verherrlichten Sohn.
Siehe! Da weinen die Götter, es weinen die Göttinnen alle,
  Daß das Schöne vergeht, daß das Vollkommene stirbt.
Auch ein Klaglied zu sein im Mund der Geliebten, ist herrlich,
  Denn das Gemeine geht klanglos zum Orkus hinab.

NENIA

Also the beautiful dies. – Its spell binds all men and immortals
    Save one: the Stygian Zeus. Armored in steel is his breast.
Once, only did soften a lover the ruler of Hades.
    Yet, ere the threshold was reached, sternly he canceled his gift.
As Aphrodite stills not the gaping wounds of Adonis
    Which on the beautiful youth, hunted, the wild boar inflicts,
So the immortal Thetis saves not her divine son Achilles
    When at the Scaean Gate, falling, he meets with his fate.
But from the sea she arises with all the daughters of Nereus,
    And they intone their lament for her transfigured son.
Lo, all the gods now are weeping and weeping is every goddess
    That the beautiful wanes, that the perfect must die.
Glory is also to be a song of sorrow of loved ones,
    For, what is vulgar goes down songless to echoless depths.

Alexander Gode

Friedrich Hölderlin

MENSCHENBEIFALL

Ist nicht heilig mein Herz, schöneren Lebens voll,
Seit ich liebe? warum achtetet ihr mich mehr,
Da ich stolzer und wilder,
Wortereicher und leerer war?

Ach! der Menge gefällt, was auf den Marktplatz taugt,
Und es ehret der Knecht nur den Gewaltsamen;
An das Göttliche glauben
Die allein, die es selber sind.

THE CROWD'S ACCLAIM

Is not my heart hallowed and filled with truer life
Since love came? Then why did ye value me more
When I was prouder and fiercer
Fuller of words, and emptier?

Yes – the crowds prefer what shines in the marketplace,
The menial eagerly crawls before the blusterer;
In the godly believe
Only those who are so themselves.

Martin Zwart

SOKRATES UND ALKIBIADES

„Warum huldigest du, heiliger Sokrates,
Diesem Jünglinge stets? Kennest du Größers nicht?
  Warum siehet mit Liebe,
    Wie auf Götter, dein Aug auf ihn?"

Wer das Tiefste gedacht, liebt das Lebendigste.
Hohe Tugend versteht, wer in die Welt geblickt,
  Und es neigen die Weisen
    Oft am Ende zu Schönem sich.

SOCRATES AND ALCIBIADES

Saintly Socrates, why do you favor
This youth incessantly? Know you nothing greater?
Why does your eye fasten
On him as on the gods with love?

Who most deeply has thought loves what is most alive;
High virtue he understands who on the world has gazed;
And often the sages
In the end bow to loveliness.

Palmer Hilty

ABENDPHANTASIE

Vor seiner Hütte ruhig im Schatten sitzt
Der Pflüger, dem Genügsamen raucht sein Herd.
Gastfreundlich tönt dem Wanderer im
Friedlichen Dorfe die Abendglocke.

Wohl kehren jetzt die Schiffer zum Hafen auch,
In fernen Städten fröhlich verrauscht des Markts
Geschäft'ger Lärm; in stiller Laube
Glänzt das gesellige Mahl den Freunden.

Wohin denn ich? Es leben die Sterblichen
Von Lohn und Arbeit; wechselnd in Müh' and Ruh'
Ist alles freudig; warum schläft denn
Nimmer nur mir in der Brust der Stachel?

Am Abendhimmel blühet ein Frühling auf;
Unzählig blühen die Rosen, und ruhig scheint
Die goldne Welt; o dorthin nehmt mich,
Purpurne Wolken! und möge droben

In Licht und Luft zerrinnen mir Lieb und Leid! –
Doch, wie verscheucht von törichter Bitte, flieht
Der Zauber; dunkel wird's, und einsam
Unter dem Himmel, wie immer, bin ich. –

Komm du nun, sanfter Schlummer! zu viel begehrt
Das Herz; doch endlich, Jugend, verglühst du ja,
Du ruhelose, träumerische!
Friedlich und heiter ist dann das Alter.

EVENING FANCY

The plowman sits in front of his shaded cot,
While evening smoke goes up from his frugal hearth.
The bell's note from the peaceful village
Rings friendly welcome to the traveller.

The boatmen doubtless now are returning too
To harbor, while in distant cities the busy hum
Of markets dies away; a friendly
Meal is laid out under quiet leafage.

But where shall I go? Men live alone by work
And wages, find their happiness turn by turn
In toil and rest; then why in my heart
Is there no sleep for the goad that pricks me?

A springtime blossoms now in the evening sky;
Unnumbered roses blossom, the golden world
Seems all at rest; oh, purple cloud banks,
Take me up there, and in light and ether

Let love and pain dissolve, and be swept away!
But now as though dispelled by my foolish prayer
The magic flees; night falls, and lonely
Under the heavens I stand, as always.

Then *you* come, gentle sleep! For my heart desires
Too much. But youth, your fire must at last burn out,
You never-resting, ardent dreamer!
Peaceful and cheerful old age comes after.

W. Edward Brown

HYPERIONS SCHICKSALSLIED

Ihr wandelt droben im Licht
Auf weichem Boden, selige Genien !
Glänzende Götterlüfte
Rühren euch leicht,
Wie die Finger der Künstlerin
Heilige Saiten.

Schicksallos, wie der schlafende
Säugling, atmen die Himmlischen;
Keusch bewahrt
In bescheidener Knospe,
Blühet ewig
Ihnen der Geist,
Und die seligen Augen
Blicken in stiller
Ewiger Klarheit.

Doch uns ist gegeben,
Auf keiner Stätte zu ruhn,
Es schwinden, es fallen
Die leidenden Menschen
Blindlings von einer
Stunde zur andern,
Wie Wasser von Klippe
Zu Klippe geworfen,
Jahrlang ins Ungewisse hinab.

HYPERION'S SONG OF FATE

You roam above in the light
On yielding meadows, blessed genii!
Brilliant ethereal breezes
Gently caress you
As by virginal fingering
Of sanctified strings.

Fatelessly, like the slumbering
Suckling breathe the celestials;
Chastely sheathed
In most modest petals
Blooms their never-
Withering spirit,
And their blissful eyes
Gaze with serene
Eternal clarity.

To us, though, is granted
No place to find for repose;
The suffering human beings
Fall and vanish,
Blind things from one hour
On to another,
As waters are hurled
From boulder to boulder
Down through the years to nowhere known.

Philip Allan Friedman

AN DIE PARZEN

Nur einen Sommer gönnt, ihr Gewaltigen!
Und einen Herbst zu reifem Gesange mir,
  Daß williger mein Herz, vom süßen
    Spiele gesättigt, dann mir sterbe!

Die Seele, der im Leben ihr göttlich Recht
Nicht ward, sie ruht auch drunten im Orkus nicht;
  Doch ist mir einst das Heilge, das am
    Herzen mir liegt, das Gedicht, gelungen:

Willkommen dann, o Stille der Schattenwelt!
Zufrieden bin ich, wenn auch mein Saitenspiel
  Mich nicht hinabgeleitet: einmal
    Lebt ich wie Götter, und mehr bedarfs nicht.

TO THE PARCAE

A single summer grant me, ye Mighty Ones!,
And time wherein to harvest the ripened song,
That willingly my heart, thus slaked in
Rhythmical sweetness may heed the Summons.

The soul whose godlike due is denied it in
This life, finds no repose in the realm of shades.
Yet once the sacred trust I have at
Heart is accomplished – the poem spoken –

Be welcome then, O quiet land of death.
At peace I rest, albeit my lyre cannot
Go with me down to Orcus. Once I
Lived like the gods, and nought else is needed.

Alexander Gode

HÄLFTE DES LEBENS

Mit gelben Birnen hänget
Und voll mit wilden Rosen
Das Land in den See,
Ihr holden Schwäne,
Und trunken von Küssen
Tunkt ihr das Haupt
Ins heilignüchterne Wasser.

Weh mir, wo nehm ich, wenn
Es Winter ist, die Blumen, und wo
Den Sonnenschein
Und Schatten der Erde?
Die Mauern stehn
Sprachlos und kalt, im Winde
Klirren die Fahnen.

HALF OF LIFE

Filled with yellow pears
And with wild roses,
The landscape hangs in the lake,
O gentle swans;
And drunk with kisses
You dip your heads
In the sacred sober water.

Alas, whence shall I take,
When it is winter, flowers and
Whence sunshine
And shadows on the ground?
The walls stand
Dumb and cold, the weathercocks
Whirr in the wind.

Willard R. Trask
Alexander Gode

DER TOD

Er erschreckt uns,
Unser Retter der Tod. Sanft kommt er
Leis im Gewölke des Schlafs.

Aber er bleibt fürchterlich, und wir sehn nur
Nieder ins Grab, ob er gleich uns zur Vollendung
Führt aus Hüllen der Nacht hinüber
In der Erkenntnisse Land.

DEATH

He frightens us,
Our Deliverer Death. Softly he comes
Faint in the clouds of sleep.

But he remains frightful, and we look only
Down into the grave, though he lead us to the summit
Out of the veil of night, over
To the land of perception.

Lyn Goetze Snyder

Unbekannter Dichter

Ich hab die Nacht geträumet
Wohl einen schweren Traum;
Es wuchs in meinem Garten
Ein Rosmarienbaum.

Der Kirchhof war der Garten,
Das Blumenbeet ein Grab,
Und von dem grünen Baume
Fiel Kron und Blüten ab.

Die Blüten tät ich sammeln
In einen goldnen Krug;
Der fiel mir aus den Händen,
Daß er in Stücke schlug.

Draus sah ich Perlen rinnen
Und Tröpflein rosenrot.
Was mag der Traum bedeuten?
Herzliebster, bist du tot?

Last night while I was dreaming
A nightmare haunted me;
I dreamed that in my garden
There grew a rosemary tree.

The garden was a graveyard,
A flowerbed the tomb,
And from the green tree falling
Came leaves, and flowers in bloom.

I gathered up the blossoms
Into a jug of gold.
It fell out of my fingers
And shattered a hundredfold.

I saw pearls running from it,
And droplets rosy red.
Ah, what can be the meaning?
My sweetest, are you dead?

D. G. Wright

Clemens Brentano

WIEGENLIED

Singet leise, leise, leise,
Singt ein flüsternd Wiegenlied,
Von dem Monde lernt die Weise,
Der so still am Himmel zieht.

Singt ein Lied so süß gelinde,
Wie die Quellen auf den Kieseln,
Wie die Bienen um die Linde
Summen, murmeln, flüstern, rieseln.

SLUMBER SONG

Softly, softly, sing a tune;
Sing a whispered lullaby;
Learn thy lay from Lady Moon,
Moving soundless through the sky.

Sing a song as sweetly sighing
As the springs on pebbles curling,
As the bees round linden flying
Humming, trickling, rustling, purling.

Anne Jennings

ABENDSTÄNDCHEN

Hör, es klagt die Flöte wieder
Und die kühlen Brunnen rauschen,
Golden wehn die Töne nieder –
Stille, stille, lass uns lauschen!

Holdes Bitten, mild Verlangen,
Wie es süß zum Herzen spricht!
Durch die Nacht, die mich umfangen,
Blickt zu mir der Töne Licht.

SERENADE

Hark, once more the flute's complaining,
And the rustling fountains glisten;
Golden strains are wafted downward –
Quiet, quiet! let us listen!

Gracious pleading, gentle longing,
To my heart they make their plea,
Through the dense night that surrounds me,
Light of music shines on me.

Anne Jennings

DER SPINNERIN LIED

Es sang vor langen Jahren
Wohl auch die Nachtigall,
Das war wohl süßer Schall,
Da wir zusammen waren.

Ich sing und kann nicht weinen
Und spinne so allein
Den Faden klar und rein,
Solang der Mond wird scheinen.

Da wir zusammen waren,
Da sang die Nachtigall,
Nun mahnet mich ihr Schall,
Daß du von mir gefahren.

So oft der Mond mag scheinen,
Gedenk ich dein allein,
Mein Herz ist klar und rein,
Gott wolle uns vereinen!

Seit du von mir gefahren,
Singt stets die Nachtigall,
Ich denk bei ihrem Schall,
Wie wir zusammen waren.

Gott wolle uns vereinen,
Hier spinn ich so allein,
Der Mond scheint klar und rein,
Ich sing und möchte weinen!

THE SPINSTRESS' SONG

Of yore, as now, aringing
Sweet sang the nightingale.
We heard the echo trail,
Each to the other clinging.

I sing to keep from weeping
And spin, all lonesome here,
The thread so pure and clear
Until the moon sets, sleeping.

Each to the other clinging
We heard the nightingale.
But now the echoes trail,
For you did leave me, singing.

Ere yet the moon sets sleeping,
My thoughts roam far from here.
My heart is pure and clear.
God join us in His keeping.

Since you did leave me, singing,
I hear the nightingale.
We heard the echoes trail,
Faintly together clinging.

God join us in His keeping.
I spin, all lonesome here,
The moon shines pure and clear,
I sing and would be weeping.

Alexander Gode

Ludwig Uhland

DES KNABEN BERGLIED

Ich bin vom Berg der Hirtenknab',
Seh' auf die Schlösser all herab;
Die Sonne strahlt am ersten hier,
Am längsten weilet sie bei mir;
Ich bin der Knab' vom Berge!

Hier ist des Stromes Mutterhaus,
Ich trink' ihn frisch vom Stein heraus;
Er braust vom Fels in wildem Lauf,
Ich fang' ihn mit den Armen auf;
Ich bin der Knab' vom Berge!

Der Berg, der ist mein Eigentum,
Da ziehn die Stürme rings herum;
Und heulen sie von Nord und Süd,
So überschallt sie doch mein Lied:
Ich bin der Knab' vom Berge!

Sind Blitz und Donner unter mir,
So steh' ich hoch im Blauen hier;
Ich kenne sie und rufe zu:
„Laßt meines Vaters Haus in Ruh'!"
Ich bin der Knab' vom Berge!

Und wann die Sturmglock' einst erschallt,
Manch Feuer auf den Bergen wallt,
Dann steig' ich nieder, tret' ins Glied
Und schwing' mein Schwert und sing' mein Lied:
Ich bin der Knab' vom Berge!

THE LAD OF THE MOUNTAIN

I stand up here where storm winds blow,
Look on the castles down below;
I see the rising sun's first gleams,
I see its latest dying beams;
I am the lad of the mountain.

The stream's maternal home is here,
I drink its freshness crystal clear;
In wild career it bursts its bands,
I catch it when I fill my hands;
I am the lad of the mountain.

The mountain is my very own,
The storm clouds round about are blown;
Though winds from north and south may roar,
My song's but louder than before;
I am the lad of the mountain.

When lightning I can see below,
And thunder hear, 'tis then I know
I'm in the clear, blue sky and cry:
"Leave us in peace as you pass by"!
I am the lad of the mountain!

But when alarm bells warning ring,
When fires from the hilltops spring,
Then I'll go down my friends among,
And swing my sword and sing my song:
I am the lad of the mountain!

Francis Owen

FRÜHLINGSGLAUBE

Die linden Lüfte sind erwacht,
Sie säuseln und weben Tag und Nacht,
Sie schaffen an allen Enden.
O frischer Duft, o neuer Klang!
Nun, armes Herze, sei nicht bang!
Nun muß sich alles, alles wenden.

Die Welt wird schöner mit jedem Tag,
Man weiß nicht, was noch werden mag,
Das Blühen will nicht enden.
Es blüht das fernste, tiefste Tal:
Nun, armes Herz, vergiß der Qual!
Nun muß sich alles, alles wenden!

HOPE IN SPRINGTIME

The balmy breezes are aloft,
By day and night are wafting soft,
From near to far they range.
What fragrance, what new sound are here!
Hush, my poor heart, be without fear!
For now it all, it all must change.

The world grows fairer every day,
What's yet to come one cannot say,
It blooms in endless range:
Blooms deck the farthest dell and plain.
Hush, my poor heart, forget thy pain!
For now it all, it all must change.

Martin Zwart

AUF DEN TOD EINES KINDES

Du kamst, du gingst mit leiser Spur,
Ein flücht'ger Gast im Erdenland;
Woher? Wohin? Wir wissen nur :
Aus Gottes Hand in Gottes Hand.

"ON THE DEATH OF A CHILD"

You came, you went, a fleeting guest
Upon the earth you lightly trod.
From where to where? We only know:
From God into the hands of God.

Oliver Brown

Josef von Eichendorff

DER FROHE WANDERSMANN

Wem Gott will rechte Gunst erweisen,
Den schickt er in die weite Welt;
Dem will er seine Wunder weisen
In Berg und Wald und Strom und Feld.

Die Trägen, die zu Hause liegen,
Erquicket nicht das Morgenrot;
Sie wissen nur von Kinderwiegen,
Von Sorgen, Last und Not um Brot.

Die Bächlein von den Bergen springen,
Die Lerchen schwirren hoch vor Lust,
Was sollt ich nicht mit ihnen singen
Aus voller Kehl und frischer Brust?

Den lieben Gott laß ich nur walten;
Der Bächlein, Lerchen, Wald und Feld
Und Erd und Himmel will erhalten,
Hat auch mein Sach aufs best bestellt!

THE JOYFUL TRAVELLER

The man whom God will show true favor,
He ushers forth to live his dream;
He gives Him all his best to savor
In wood and hill and field and stream.

The rosy dawn can never thrill them,
Those lazy souls who lie abed.
Their lives? Why, rocking cradles fill them,
And troubles, cares, and need for bread.

The brooks go leaping down the mountain,
The larks whir high to show their art;
Why can't my song burst from the fountain
Of my full throat and happy heart?

The ruling power, to God reserve it;
The brook, the lark, the field, the wood,
The earth, the sky, He will preserve it,
And guide my life to make it good.

Stewart H. Benedict

DER EINSIEDLER

Komm, Trost der Welt, du stille Nacht!
Wie steigst du von den Bergen sacht,
Die Lüfte alle schlafen.
Ein Schiffer nur noch, wandermüd,
Singt übers Meer sein Abendlied
Zu Gottes Lob im Hafen.

Die Jahre wie die Wolken gehn
Und lassen mich hier einsam stehn,
Die Welt hat mich vergessen,
Da tratst du wunderbar zu mir,
Wenn ich beim Waldesrauschen hier
Gedankenvoll gesessen.

O Trost der Welt, du stille Nacht!
Der Tag hat mich so müd gemacht,
Das weite Meer schon dunkelt,
Laß ausruhn mich von Lust und Not,
Bis daß das ew'ge Morgenrot
Den stillen Wald durchfunkelt.

THE HERMIT

Balm of the world, come, quiet night!
Thou sinkest from the mountains' height,
The evening winds are sleeping.
A sailor only, travel-worn,
Sings cross the port alone, forlorn,
His praise for God's safekeeping.

Like drifting clouds the years roll by.
Forgotten by the world stand I
Alone in all creation.
But oft thy comfort came to me
When underneath a rustling tree
I sat in contemplation.

Balm of the world, thou quiet night!
I'm wearied by the day's great might,
The wide, wide sea is darkling,
Grant me to rest from joy and woe
Till the eternal morning glow
Sets the dark forest sparkling.

Meno Spann

MONDNACHT

Es war, als hätt der Himmel
Die Erde still geküßt,
Daß sie im Blütenschimmer
Von ihm nun träumen müßt.

Die Luft ging durch die Felder,
Die Ähren wogten sacht,
Es rauschten leis die Wälder,
So sternklar war die Nacht.

Und meine Seele spannte
Weit ihre Flügel aus,
Flog durch die stillen Lande,
Als flöge sie nach Haus.

MOONLIT NIGHT

The sky had kissed the earth to sleep
So silently, 'twould seem,
That in her flowering glory she
Of him alone would dream.

Across the fields the playful breeze
The corn ears softly swayed,
A gentle whisper stirred the trees,
The night for stars was made.

My soul stretched out its yearning wings,
As far and wide to roam,
Flew through the quiet countryside,
As though 'twere flying home.

D. G. Wright

DIE NACHTBLUME

Nacht ist wie ein stilles Meer,
Lust und Leid und Liebesklagen
Kommen so verworren her
In dem linden Wellenschlagen.

Wünsche wie die Wolken sind,
Schiffen durch die stillen Räume,
Wer erkennt im lauen Wind,
Obs Gedanken oder Träume? –

Schließ ich nun auch Herz und Mund,
Die so gern den Sternen klagen:
Leise doch im Herzensgrund
Bleibt das linde Wellenschlagen.

NIGHT

Night is like a silent sea,
Joy and pain and love's sad urging
Reach us so confusedly
Through the gentle wavelet's surging.

Wishes like light clouds afloat,
Through the quiet spaces drifting,
In this soft wind who can note
If they're thoughts or dream-wraiths shifting?

If I silence voice and heart,
Which would cry out vainly urging
To the stars, still deep apart
Sounds that gentle wavelets' surging.

Isabel S. MacInnes

WALDGESPRÄCH

Es ist schon spät, es wird schon kalt,
Was reitst du einsam durch den Wald?
Der Wald ist lang, du bist allein,
Du schöne Braut! Ich führ dich heim!

„Groß ist der Männer Trug und List,
Vor Schmerz mein Herz gebrochen ist,
Wohl irrt das Waldhorn her und hin,
O flieh! Du weißt nicht, wer ich bin.‟

So reich geschmückt ist Roß und Weib,
So wunderschön der junge Leib,
Jetzt kenn ich dich—Gott steh mir bei!
Du bist die Hexe Lorelei.

„Du kennst mich wohl—von hohem Stein
Schaut still mein Schloß tief in den Rhein.
Es ist schon spät, es wird schon kalt,
Kommst nimmermehr aus diesem Wald!‟

DIALOGUE IN THE FOREST

"The hour is late, the sun is gone.
Why are you riding here alone?
The woodland's wide, I'll be your guide
And lead you home, my lovely bride!"

"Men's falseness and deceit are great;
Crushed is my heart beneath grief's weight.
The hunting horn sounds far and near—
Oh flee if life you cherish dear!"

"Your splendid steed, your dazzling dress,
Your body's young seductiveness—
I know you now! God hear my cry!
You are the sorceress Lorelei!"

"You know me well—a castle's mine
That towers high above the Rhine.
The hour is late, chill grows the eve.
This forest you shall never leave!"

Gerd Gillhoff

WÜNSCHELRUTE

Schläft ein Lied in allen Dingen,
Die da träumen fort und fort,
Und die Welt hebt an zu singen,
Triffst du nur das Zauberwort.

WISHING WAND

Slumb'ring deep in every thing
Dreams a song as yet unheard,
And the world begins to sing
If you find the magic word.

Alison Turner

Wilhelm Müller

WANDERSCHAFT

Das Wandern ist des Müllers Lust,
Das Wandern!
Das muß ein schlechter Müller sein,
Dem niemals fiel das Wandern ein,
Das Wandern!

Vom Wasser haben wir's gelernt,
Vom Wasser!
Das hat nicht Rast bei Tag und Nacht,
Ist stets auf Wanderschaft bedacht,
Das Wasser!

Das sehn wir auch den Rädern ab,
Den Rädern!
Die gar nicht gerne stille stehn,
Die sich mein Tag nicht müde drehn.
Die Räder!

Die Steine selbst, so schwer sie sind,
Die Steine!
Sie tanzen mit den muntern Reihn
Und wollen gar noch schneller sein,
Die Steine!

O Wandern, Wandern, meine Lust,
O Wandern!
Herr Meister und Frau Meisterin,
Laßt mich in Friede weiter ziehn
Und wandern!

THE JOURNEYMAN'S SONG

Oh wandering is a miller's joy,
Oh wandering!
He must a sorry miller be
Who never wanted to be free
For wandering!

The water taught us what to do,
The water!
For it rests not by night or day,
And always strains to be away,
The water!

We learn it from the millwheels too,
The millwheels!
They're like the water down below,
I've never seen them weary grow,
The millwheels!

The millstones too, though heavy they,
The millstones!
In merry circles round they dance,
Would like to faster race and prance,
The millstones!

Oh wandering, wandering, my delight,
Oh wandering!
Oh master, mistress Miller, pray
Let me in peace now go away
And wander!

Francis Owen

DER LINDENBAUM

Am Brunnen vor dem Tore
Da steht ein Lindenbaum:
Ich träumt in seinem Schatten
So manchen süßen Traum.
Ich schnitt in seine Rinde
So manches liebe Wort;
Es zog in Freud und Leide
Zu ihm mich immer fort.

Ich mußt auch heute wandern
Vorbei in tiefer Nacht,
Da hab ich noch im Dunkel
Die Augen zugemacht.
Und seine Zweige rauschten,
Als riefen sie mir zu:
Komm her zu mir, Geselle,
Hier findst du deine Ruh!

Die kalten Winde bliesen
Mir grad ins Angesicht,
Der Hut flog mir vom Kopfe
Ich wendete mich nicht.
Nun bin ich manche Stunde
Entfernt von jenem Ort,
Und immer hör ichs rauschen:
Du fändest Ruhe dort!

AT THE FOUNTAIN BY THE GATEWAY

At fountain by the gateway
A lime tree's standing there;
I've dreamt within its shadow
Full many a dream so fair;
I've cut into its surface
Full many a loving word;
In joy and sorrow ever
Its call to me I've heard.

And still today in passing
At dead of night along,
I closed my eyes and listened
Those memories among;
And I could hear the branches,
As if they called to me:
Come back to me, old comrade,
And from your grief be free!

The chilling winds were blowing
Direct into my face;
My hat flew off and vanished,
I did not leave the place.
And now full many an hour
Away from that lime tree,
I hear it ever rustling:
You would have here been free!

Francis Owen

Heinrich Heine

Leise zieht durch mein Gemüt
Liebliches Geläute,
Klinge, kleines Frühlingslied,
Kling' hinaus ins Weite.

Kling' hinaus bis an das Haus,
Wo die Blumen sprießen.
Wenn du eine Rose schaust,
Sag' ich lass' sie grüßen.

Softly through my spirit flow
Melodies entreating;
Fill the air with songs and go,
Bear my springtime greeting.

Sing my lay where flowers gay
Deck a house you're meeting;
If you see a rose that way,
Say, I send her greeting.

Francis Owen

Es war ein alter König,
Sein Herz war schwer, sein Haupt war grau;
Der arme, alte König,
Er nahm eine junge Frau.

Es war ein schöner Page,
Blond war sein Haupt, leicht war sein Sinn;
Er trug die seidne Schleppe
Der jungen Königin.

Kennst du das alte Liedchen?
Es klingt so süß, es klingt so trüb!
Sie mußten beide sterben,
Sie hatten sich viel zu lieb.

There was an aged monarch,
His heart was grave, his hair was gray;
This poor old monarch married
A maid that was young and gay.

There was a handsome page-boy,
Blond was his hair, bright was his mien;
He bore the silken train
Of this so youthful queen.

You know this old, old story?
It sounds so sweet, so sad to tell!
The lovers had to perish,
They loved each other too well.

Karl Weimar

Ein Fichtenbaum steht einsam
Im Norden auf kahler Höh.
Ihn schläfert; mit weißer Decke
Umhüllen ihn Eis und Schnee.

Er träumt von einer Palme,
Die, fern im Morgenland,
Einsam und schweigend trauert
Auf brennender Felsenwand.

A fir tree standing lonely
On a windswept northern height
Slumbered under the icy
Covering of white;

Slumbered and dreamed of a palm tree
Far in an Orient land,
Lonely and silent mourning
On a cliff of burning sand.

Margaret R. Richter

DIE WANDERRATTEN

Es gibt zwei Sorten Ratten:
Die hungrigen und satten.
Die satten bleiben vergnügt zu Haus,
Die hungrigen aber wandern aus.

Sie wandern viel tausend Meilen,
Ganz ohne Rasten und Weilen,
Gradaus in ihrem grimmigen Lauf,
Nicht Wind noch Wetter hält sie auf.

Sie klimmen wohl über die Höhen,
Sie schwimmen wohl durch die Seen;
Gar manche ersäuft oder bricht das Genick,
Die lebenden lassen die toten zurück.

Es haben diese Käuze
Gar fürchterliche Schnäuze;
Sie tragen die Köpfe geschoren egal,
Ganz radikal, ganz rattenkahl.

Die radikale Rotte
Weiß nichts von einem Gotte.
Sie lassen nicht taufen ihre Brut,
Die Weiber sind Gemeindegut.

THE WANDERING RATS

There are two sorts of rat:
The hungry and the fat.
Content, the fat ones stay at home,
But hungry rats get out and roam.

They wander mile on mile,
They never rest awhile.
No wind or weather can hold back
That furious and untiring pack.

No mountain is too steep,
No ocean is too deep.
Many are drowned or break their heads,
The living march and leave the dead.

They have, these awful louts,
Most fearful-looking snouts.
Like Roundheads they all crop their hair,
Their Radical ratty call fills the air.

There is no Radical Red
Who's heard of the Godhead.
Baptism's a rite their brats don't see,
Their wives are common property.

Der sinnliche Rattenhaufen,
Er will nur fressen und saufen,
Er denkt nicht, während er säuft und frißt,
Daß unsre Seele unsterblich ist.

So eine wilde Ratze,
Die fürchtet nicht Hölle, nicht Katze;
Sie hat kein Gut, sie hat kein Geld
Und wünscht aufs neue zu teilen die Welt.

Die Wanderratten, o wehe!
Sie sind schon in der Nähe.
Sie rücken heran, ich höre schon
Ihr Pfeifen—die Zahl ist Legion.

O wehe! wir sind verloren,
Sie sind schon vor den Toren!
Der Bürgermeister und Senat,
Sie schütteln die Köpfe, und keiner weiß Rat.

Die Bürgeschaft greift zu den Waffen,
Die Glocken läuten die Pfaffen.
Gefährdet ist das Palladium
Des sittlichen Staats, das Eigentum.

That sensual crowd can think
Only of food and drink.
They pause not to reflect at all
Upon our everlasting soul.

That's them, those savage rats
Who fear not hell nor cats.
They have no land, no cash, and wish
The whole world to share out afresh.

The wandering rats, I hear—
And now it seems so near—
Their piping: they are marching on,
Their number must be legion.

Alas, it is too late,
They're knocking at the gate!
The mayor and the corporation
Shake their heads in consternation.

The burghers fly to arms,
The priests ring loud alarms,
The Palladium is in jeopardy—
Morality, state, and property.

Nicht Glockengeläute, nicht Pfaffengebete,
Nicht hochwohlweise Senatsdekrete,
Auch nicht Kanonen, viel Hundertpfünder,
Sie helfen euch heute, ihr lieben Kinder!

Heut helfen euch nicht die Wortgespinste
Der abgelebten Redekünste.
Man fängt nicht Ratten mit Syllogismen,
Sie springen über die feinsten Sophismen.

Im hungrigen Magen Eingang finden
Nur Suppenlogik mit Knödelgründen,
Nur Argumente von Rinderbraten,
Begleitet von Göttinger Wurstzitaten.

Ein schweigender Stockfisch, in Butter gesotten,
Behaget den radikalen Rotten
Viel besser als ein Mirabeau
Und alle Redner seit Cicero.

No prayer of priest, no clanging bell,
No senate's decree, though drafted so well,
No cannon, not a hundred-pounder,
Can save you, children, from this danger.

No fine-spun words can help you now
Nor tricks of rhetoric, I vow.
You can't catch rats with syllogisms,
They spring clean over all sophisms.

In hungry mouths enters alone
Logic of soup, grounded in bone,
Such arguments as chunks of beef,
With sausages to seal belief.

Silent cod with butter and bread
Can move that kind of Radical Red
More deeply than a Mirabeau
Or any speaker since Cicero.

Charles Issawi

DIE ROSE, DIE LILIE, DIE TAUBE, DIE SONNE

Die Rose, die Lilie, die Taube, die Sonne,
Die liebt ich einst alle in Liebeswonne.
Ich lieb sie nicht mehr, ich liebe alleine
Die Kleine, die Feine, die Reine, die Eine;
Sie selber, aller Liebe Bronne,
Ist Rose und Lilie und Taube und Sonne.

THE ROSE, THE LILY, THE DOVE, THE SUN

The rose and the lily, the sun and the dove,
I loved them all once, with the rapture of love.
I love them no longer, I love one alone,
The pure one, the dear one, the fair one, my own,
The fountain of love, from whom all love flows—
My lily, my sun, my dove and my rose.

Charles Issawi

WO?

Wo wird einst des Wandermüden
Letzte Ruhestätte sein?
Unter Palmen in dem Süden?
Unter Linden an dem Rhein?

Werd' ich wo in einer Wüste
Eingescharrt von fremder Hand?
Oder ruh' ich an der Küste
Eines Meeres in dem Sand?

Immerhin! Mich wird umgeben
Gotteshimmel, dort wie hier,
Und als Totenlampen schweben
Nachts die Sterne über mir.

WHERE?

What last resting place awaits me
When this weary journey's done?
By the Rhine, beneath the lime trees?
Under palms and southern sun?

Will some stranger's hand inter me
In the desert's shifting sand?
Shall I rest beside the ocean
On some seacoast's salty strand?

Yet God's sky will be above me
Still, no matter where I lie.
And at night the stars will hang there,
Funeral candles in the sky.

Helen Sebba

Ich hatte einst ein schönes Vaterland.
Der Eichenbaum
Wuchs dort so hoch, die Veilchen nickten sanft,
Es war ein Traum.

Das küßte mich auf deutsch und sprach auf deutsch
(Man glaubt es kaum
Wie gut es klang) das Wort: „Ich liebe dich!"
Es war ein Traum.

I used to have the fairest fatherland.
The oak trees there
Were tall, so tall; the violets soft and blue.
A dream – so fair.

The kisses were in German and the word –
Strange though it seem,
It rang so true – the word: Ich liebe dich.
A dream, a dream.

Alexander Gode

Friedrich Hauff

REITERS MORGENGESANG

Morgenrot,
Leuchtest mir zum frühen Tod?
Bald wird die Trompete blasen,
Dann muß ich mein Leben lassen,
Ich und mancher Kamerad.

Kaum gedacht,
Ward der Lust ein End gemacht!
Gestern noch auf stolzen Rossen,
Heute durch die Brust geschossen,
Morgen in das kühle Grab.

Ach, wie bald
Schwindet Schönheit und Gestalt!
Prahlst du gleich mit deinen Wangen,
Die wie Milch und Purpur prangen?
Ach, die Rosen welken all!

Darum still
Füg ich mich, wie Gott es will.
Nun, so will ich wacker streiten
Und sollt ich den Tod erleiden,
Stirbt ein wackrer Reitersmann.

SONG BEFORE THE BATTLE

Blush of dawn!
Has my time on earth then gone?
Soon the bugle will be blowing,
Soon my life-blood will be flowing,
Mine and many a comrade's too!

Scarce begun,
Till the sands of life are run;
Yesterday on horses flying,
Now mid hail of bullets dying,
Soon then in the cold, cold grave!

Soon, alas,
Lovely form and beauty pass;
Cheeks today so proudly glowing,
Boastful health and color showing!
Roses wither soon and die!

But be still,
Life will go as fate may will;
So I'll try to bravely meet it,
Even death and bravely greet it
Like a valiant cavalier.

Francis Owen

Nikolaus Lenau

AN DIE ENTFERNTE

Diese Rose pflück ich hier,
In der fremden Ferne;
Liebes Mädchen, dir, ach dir
Brächt ich sie so gerne!

Doch bis ich zu dir mag ziehn
Viele weite Meilen,
Ist die Rose längst dahin,
Denn die Rosen eilen.

Nie soll weiter sich ins Land
Lieb von Liebe wagen,
Als sich blühend in der Hand
Läßt die Rose tragen;

Oder als die Nachtigall
Halme bringt zum Neste,
Oder als ihr süßer Schall
Wandert mit dem Weste.

TO HER FAR AWAY

Here in foreign land this rose
I have gathered sadly
And would take this rose I chose
To you, dear girl, gladly.

But ere back to you I fly
Over hill and valley,
Wither will the rose and die;
Roses cannot dally.

Let not ever farther stray
Love from love and lover
Than a rose in bloom will stay,
In a cupped hand's cover,

Than a nesting nightingale
Roams for twigs and grasses,
Than its song down through the vale
With the west wind passes.

Alexander Gode

AUF EINE HOLLÄNDISCHE LANDSCHAFT

Müde schleichen hier die Bäche,
Nicht ein Lüftchen hörst du wallen,
Die entfärbten Blätter fallen
Still zu Grund vor Altersschwäche.

Krähen, kaum die Schwingen regend,
Streichen langsam; dort am Hügel
Läßt die Windmühl' ruhn die Flügel;
Ach, wie schläfrig ist die Gegend!

Lenz und Sommer sind verflogen;
Dort das Hüttlein, ob es trutze,
Blickt nicht aus, die Strohkapuze
Tief ins Aug' herabgezogen.

Schlummernd oder träge sinnend
Ruht der Hirt bei seinen Schafen.
Die Natur, Herbstnebel spinnend,
Scheint am Rocken eingeschlafen.

TO A DUTCH LANDSCAPE

Weary is the brooklet's flow,
Here is heard no wand'ring breeze;
Leaves fall softly from the trees,
Tired and pale, to earth below.

Crows, whose wings move but a trace,
Fly so slowly; on the hill
Windmill arms are resting, still,
Oh, how sleepy is this place!

Spring and summer have flown by;
There the hut, as if in spite,
Has its straw hat, shunning light,
Drawn down far below its eye.

Dozing through the idle days,
Lies the shepherd by his sheep.
Nature, spinning autumn haze,
Now has found forgetful sleep.

                         Roger C. Norton

SCHILFLIED (V)

Auf dem Teich, dem regungslosen,
Weilt des Mondes holder Glanz,
Flechtend seine bleichen Rosen
In des Schilfes grünen Kranz.

Hirsche wandeln dort am Hügel,
Blicken in die Nacht empor;
Manchmal regt sich das Geflügel
Träumerisch im tiefen Rohr.

Weinend muß mein Blick sich senken;
Durch die tiefste Seele geht
Mir ein süßes Deingedenken
Wie ein stilles Nachtgebet!

SONG OF THE RUSHES (V)

On the pond, which now reposes,
Moonbeams in full beauty glow,
As they plait their pallid roses
Where green wreaths of rushes grow.

On the hill the deer are roaming,
Looking upward into night;
In the rushes' restful gloaming,
Birds stir oft with dream's delight.

Tearfully my glance is falling;
Through my deepest soul's dark lair
Thoughts of you come sweetly calling
Like a quiet evening prayer.

Roger C. Norton

DIE DREI ZIGEUNER

Drei Zigeuner fand ich einmal
Liegen an einer Weide,
Als mein Fuhrwerk mit müder Qual
Schlich durch sandige Heide.

Hielt der eine für sich allein
In den Händen die Fiedel,
Spielte, umglüht vom Abendschein,
Sich ein feuriges Liedel.

Hielt der zweite die Pfeif im Mund,
Blickte nach seinem Rauche,
Froh, als ob er vom Erdenrund
Nichts zum Glücke mehr brauche.

Und der dritte behaglich schlief,
Und sein Zimbal am Baum hing,
Über die Saiten ein Windhauch lief,
Über sein Herz ein Traum ging.

An den Kleidern trugen die drei
Löcher und bunte Flicken;
Aber sie boten trotzig frei
Spott den Erdengeschicken.

Dreifach haben sie mir gezeigt,
Wenn das Leben uns nachtet,
Wie mans verraucht, verschläft, vergeigt
Und es dreimal verachtet.

Nach den Zigeunern lang noch schaun
Mußt ich im Weiterfahren,
Nach den Gesichtern dunkelbraun,
Den schwarzlockigen Haaren.

THE THREE GYPSIES

Gypsies three I found one day,
'Gainst a willow lying,
As my coach its cumbrous way
Through the heath was plying.

One of the three a fiddle bowed
For his own sweet pleasure;
While the sunset round him glowed,
Played he a fiery measure.

And the second with many a puff
Watched the smoke rings vanish,
Looking as though a pipe were enough
Cares from life to banish.

And the third one calmly slept;
From his cimbal a gleam glanced;
Over its strings the wind's breath swept,
Over his heart a dream danced.

Stains and patches their garments displayed,
Which were rent and tattered,
But their defiant looks conveyed
That only freedom mattered.

Threefold they showed me how to be gay
When by life we are daunted,
How to fiddle, smoke, sleep it away,
How it may three times be taunted.

Back at the gypsies long I gazed
From my coach's traces,
At their black locks, sunset-glazed,
At their dark brown faces.

Gerd Gillhoff

DIE DREI

Drei Reiter nach verlorner Schlacht,
Wie reiten sie so sacht, so sacht!

Aus tiefen Wunden quillt das Blut,
Es spürt das Roß die warme Flut.

Vom Sattel tropft das Blut, vom Zaun,
Und spült hinunter Staub und Schaum.

Die Rosse schreiten sanft und weich,
Sonst flöß' das Blut zu rasch, zu reich.

Die Reiter reiten dicht gesellt,
Und einer sich am andern hält.

Sie sehn sich traurig ins Gesicht,
Und einer um den andern spricht:

„Mir blüht daheim die schönste Maid,
Drum tut mein früher Tod mir leid."

„Hab' Haus und Hof und grünen Wald,
Und sterben muß ich hier so bald!"

„Den Blick hab' ich in Gottes Welt,
Sonst nichts, doch schwer mir's Sterben fällt."

Und lauernd auf den Todesritt
Ziehn durch die Luft drei Geier mit.

Sie teilen kreischend unter sich:
„Den speisest du, den du, den ich."

THE THREE

Three riders after harsh defeat,
How slowly, slowly they retreat!

From deep-cut gashes flows their blood,
The horses feel the tepid flood.

From saddle drips the blood, from rein,
And washes dust off flank and mane.

The steed's advance is gently slow,
Or else too swift the blood's rich flow.

The dying horsemen, side by side,
Clasp one another while they ride,

And each with mien disconsolate
Now mourns that this should be his fate:

"A maid has promised me her hand –
Why must I die in foreign land?"

"Have home and farm and forest green,
And meet a death so unforeseen!"

"To me life was God's only boon
But still I grieve to die so soon."

And where they on their death-ride fare,
Three vultures follow through the air.

They share the men with piercing cry:
"Him you devour, him you, him I!"

Gerd Gillhoff

BITTE

Weil auf mir, du dunkles Auge,
Übe deine ganze Macht,
Ernste, milde, träumerische,
Unergründlich süße Nacht!

Nimm mit deinem Zauberdunkel
Diese Welt von hinnen mir,
Daß du über meinem Leben
Einsam schwebest für und für.

PLEA

Rest upon me, eye of darkness,
Practice now your every might,
Never fathomed in your beauty,
Solemn, gentle, dreaming night.

By the magic of your darkness
Take from me this world away,
That above my life forever
Lonely you may keep your sway.

George C. Schoolfield

Eduard Mörike

SCHÖN-ROHTRAUT

Wie heißt König Ringangs Töchterlein?
Rohtraut, Schön-Rohtraut.
Was tut sie denn den ganzen Tag,
Da sie wohl nicht spinnen und nähen mag?
Tut fischen und jagen.
O daß ich doch ihr Jäger wär!
Fischen und Jagen freute mich sehr.
– Schweig stille, mein Herze!

Und über eine kleine Weil,
Rohtraut, Schön-Rohtraut,
So dient der Knab auf Ringangs Schloß
In Jägertracht und hat ein Roß,
Mit Rohtraut zu jagen.
O daß ich doch ein Königssohn wär!
Rohtraut, Schön-Rohtraut lieb ich so sehr.
– Schweig stille, mein Herze!

Einsmals sie ruhten am Eichenbaum,
Da lacht Schön-Rohtraut:
,,Was siehst mich an so wunniglich?
Wenn du das Herz hast, küsse mich!"
Ach! erschrak der Knabe!
Doch denket er: ,,Mir ist's vergunnt",
Und küsset Schön-Rohtraut auf den Mund.
– Schweig stille, mein Herze!

Darauf sie ritten schweigend heim,
Rohtraut, Schön-Rohtraut;
Es jauchzt der Knab in seinem Sinn!

FAIR ROHTRAUT

Oh, what is the name of King Ringang's daughter?
Rohtraut, Fair Rohtraut.
And what does she do the live-long day,
Since she scarcely would spin and knit alway?
She goes fishing and hunting.
Oh, that her huntsman I might be!
I'd fish and hunt right merrily.
– Ah, be silent, my heart!

And after just a little while,
Rohtraut, Fair Rohtraut,
The lad did serve at Ringang's court
In squire's garb and had a horse,
To hunt with Rohtraut.
Oh, that a king's son I might be!
I love Fair Rohtraut tenderly.
– Ah, be silent, my heart!

One day they stopped by an old oak tree,
Then laughed Fair Rohtraut:
"Why look at me so blissfully?
If you have courage, come, kiss me!"
Oh, how startled the lad was!
And yet he thinks: 'Twas offered me,"
And kisses Fair Rohtraut tenderly.
– Ah, be silent, my heart!

And then they rode quite silent home,
Rohtraut, Fair Rohtraut;
The lad exulted all the way:

„Und würdst du heute Kaiserin,
Mich sollt's nicht kränken !
Ihr tausend Blätter im Walde wißt,
Ich hab Schön-Rohtrauts Mund geküßt !
– Schweig stille, mein Herze!"

Though you were made an Empress today,
It would not grieve me;
Ye thousand leaves in the forest, hear!
I've kissed Fair Rohtraut's mouth so dear!
Ah, be silent, my heart!

Isabel S. MacInnes

DER GÄRTNER

Auf ihrem Leibrößlein,
So weiß wie der Schnee,
Die schönste Prinzessin
Reit't durch die Allee.

Der Weg, den das Rößlein
Hintanzet so hold,
Der Sand, den ich streute,
Er blinket wie Gold.

Du rosenfarbs Hütlein,
Wohl auf und wohl ab,
O wirf eine Feder
Verstohlen herab!

Und willst du dagegen
Eine Blüte von mir,
Nimm tausend für eine,
Nimm alle dafür!

THE GARDENER

On her fleet little charger
As white as the snow
The handsomest princess
Rides through the park row.

The path which the horse strides
So gay and so bold,
The sand that I scattered,
It sparkles like gold.

You pink-colored bonnet,
Now up and now down,
Oh throw me a feather
Clandestinely down!

And should you desire
A flower today,
Take a thousand in barter,
Take a fulsome bouquet!

Ernst Rose

DAS VERLASSENE MÄGDLEIN

Früh, wann die Hähne krähn,
Eh die Sternlein verschwinden,
Muß ich am Herde stehn,
Muß Feuer zünden.

Schön ist der Flammen Schein,
Es springen die Funken;
Ich schaue so drein,
In Leid versunken.

Plötzlich, da kommt es mir,
Treuloser Knabe,
Daß ich die Nacht von dir
Geträumet habe.

Träne auf Träne dann
Stürzet hernieder;
So kommt der Tag heran—
O ging' er wieder!

THE FORSAKEN SERVANT GIRL

Early, when the cocks crow,
Ere the little stars dwindle,
To the hearth I must go
The fire to kindle.

Beautiful is the blaze,
The sparks are flying.
Into the flames I gaze,
Woefully sighing.

Suddenly, unfaithful lad,
It comes back to me—
This very night I had
A dream of thee.

Tear, then, after tear
My face streams down.
So does the day draw near—
O would it were gone!

Gerd Gillhoff

UM MITTERNACHT

Gelassen stieg die Nacht ans Land,
Lehnt träumend an der Berge Wand,
Ihr Auge sieht die goldne Waage nun
Der Zeit in gleichen Schalen stille ruhn;
   Und kecker rauschen die Quellen hervor,
   Sie singen der Mutter, der Nacht, ins Ohr
      Vom Tage,
   Vom heute gewesenen Tage.

Das uralt alte Schlummerlied,
Sie achtets nicht, sie ist es müd;
Ihr klingt des Himmels Bläue süßer noch,
Der flücht'gen Stunden gleichgeschwungnes Joch.
   Doch immer behalten die Quellen das Wort,
   Es singen die Wasser im Schlafe noch fort
      Vom Tage,
   Vom heute gewesenen Tage.

AT MIDNIGHT

Serenely Night set foot upon the land,
Leans dreaming where the walls of mountains stand.
Her eye beholds Time's golden scales now come
To rest in silent equilibrium.
   And bolder each source gushes forth and each spring;
   In the ear of their mother, the Night, they sing
     Of the day,
   Of what was and no more is this day.

That ancient lullaby, that age-old strain—
She heeds it not, weary of its refrain.
In heaven's blue she hears a sweeter chime:
The arched-yoke symmetry of fleeting time.
   But ceaselessly whisper the sources and springs,
   And even in sleep every water still sings
     Of the day,
   Of what was and no more is this day.

Sheema Z. Buehne

VERBORGENHEIT

Laß, o Welt, o laß mich sein!
Locket nicht mit Liebesgaben,
Laßt dies Herz alleine haben
Seine Wonne, seine Pein!

Was ich traure, weiß ich nicht,
Es ist unbekanntes Wehe;
Immerdar durch Tränen sehe
Ich der Sonne liebes Licht.

Oft bin ich mir kaum bewußt,
Und die helle Freude zücket
Durch die Schwere, so mich drücket,
Wonniglich in meiner Brust.

Laß, o Welt, o laß mich sein!
Locket nicht mit Liebesgaben,
Laßt dies Herz alleine haben
Seine Wonne, seine Pein!

SECLUSION

Leave me, world, just let me go!
Tempt me not with soothing pleasure,
Leave this heart alone to treasure
All its rapture, all its woe!

Why I grieve, I do not know:
Mine is unexplained lamenting;
Still through all my senseless weeping
I behold the sun's bright glow.

Oft I feel so far apart,
And a joyful gladness draws me
Through the troubles that oppress me
Blissfully within my heart.

Leave me, world, just let me go!
Tempt me not with soothing pleasure,
Leave this heart alone to treasure
All its rapture, all its woe!

D. G. Wright

DENK ES, O SEELE!

Ein Tännlein grünet wo,
Wer weiß, im Walde,
Ein Rosenstrauch, wer sagt,
In welchem Garten?
Sie sind erlesen schon,
Denk es, o Seele!
Auf deinem Grab zu wurzeln
Und zu wachsen.

Zwei schwarze Rößlein weiden,
Auf der Wiese,
Sie kehren heim zur Stadt
In muntern Sprüngen.
Sie werden schrittweis gehn
Mit deiner Leiche;
Vielleicht, vielleicht noch eh
An ihren Hufen
Das Eisen los wird,
Das ich blitzen sehe!

THINK OF IT, MY SOUL

Green stands a fir tree, who
Knows where in the forest, –
A rosebush, who can tell
Within what garden?
They are already chosen –
Think of it, my soul –
To root themselves and grow
Upon thy grave.

Two jet-black horses pasture
On the meadow;
Home to town they come
Jauntily prancing.
At slow walk they will pace
Before thy corpse
Sooner perhaps . . . perhaps . . .
Than on their hooves
The shoe-iron loosens
Which I see flashing.

Charles E. Passage

Ferdinand Freiligrath

O lieb, so lang du lieben kannst!
O lieb, so lang du lieben magst!
Die Stunde kommt, die Stunde kommt,
Wo du an Gräbern stehst und klagst!

Und sorge, daß dein Herze glüht
Und Liebe hegt und Liebe trägt,
So lang ihm noch ein ander Herz
In Liebe warm entgegenschlägt!

Und wer dir seine Brust erschließt,
O tu ihm, was du kannst, zulieb!
Und mach ihm jede Stunde froh,
Und mach ihm keine Stunde trüb!

Und hüte deine Zunge wohl,
Bald ist ein böses Wort gesagt!
O Gott, es war nicht bös gemeint—
Der andre aber geht und klagt.

O lieb, so lang du lieben kannst!
O lieb, so lang du lieben magst!
Die Stunde kommt, die Stunde kommt,
Wo du an Gräbern stehst und klagst!

Dan kniest du nieder an der Gruft,
Und birgst die Augen, trüb und naß,
—Sie sehn den andern nimmermehr—
Ins lange, feuchte Kirchhofgras.

Oh love as long as you can love,
Love while it's given you to love,
The hour shall come, the hour shall come
When you will sob beside the grave.

And see that your heart glows with love,
If filled with love and love alone,
As long as there's another heart
Whose warm heartbeat answers your own.

And he who opens his heart to you,
Do all you can to make him glad,
And always, always, give him joy
And never, never, make him sad.

And take good care to hold your tongue—
An angry word's easy to say;
"Oh God—you know no harm was meant,"
But he was hurt, and went away.

Oh love as long as you can love,
Love while it's given you to love,
The hour shall come, the hour shall come
When you will sob beside the grave.

Then you will kneel beside the tomb,
Cast down your sad and tearful eyes.
He never will be seen again
Who in the long and damp grass lies.

Und sprichst: O schau auf mich herab,
Der hier an deinem Grabe weint!
Vergib, daß ich gekränkt dich hab!
O Gott, es war nicht bös gemeint!

Er aber sieht und hört dich nicht,
Kommt nicht, daß du ihn froh umfängst;
Der Mund, der oft dich küßte, spricht
Nie wieder: ich vergab dir längst!

Er tats, vergab dir lange schon,
Doch manche heiße Träne fiel
Um dich und um dein herbes Wort.
Doch still—er ruht, er ist am Ziel!

O lieb, so lang du lieben kannst!
O lieb, so lang du lieben magst!
Die Stunde kommt, die Stunde kommt,
Wo du an Gräbern stehst und klagst!

And say, "Oh look at me again
Who here am weeping by your grave,
Oh God, you know no harm was meant,
Forgive the sorrow that I gave."

But he can neither see nor hear,
Your warm embrace he cannot know,
The mouth that kissed you cannot say
"But I forgave you long ago!"

He did—forgive you long ago,
Though many were the tears that fell
Because of you and your harsh words—
The goal now gained he's resting well.

Oh love as long as you can love,
Love while it's given you to love,
The hour shall come, the hour shall come
When you will sob beside the grave.

Charles Issawi

Friedrich Hebbel

ICH UND DU

Wir träumten voneinander
Und sind davon erwacht,
Wir leben, um uns zu lieben,
Und sinken zurück in die Nacht.

Du tratst aus meinem Traume,
Aus deinem trat ich hervor,
Wir sterben, wenn sich Eines
Im Andern ganz verlor.

Auf einer Lilie zittern
Zwei Tropfen, rein und rund,
Zerfließen in Eins und rollen
Hinab in des Kelches Grund.

YOU AND I

We dreamed of one another
And wakened to the light;
We live to love each other
And sink back into the night.

You stepped out of my dreaming,
Out of your dream stepped I;
If either is ever wholly
Lost in the other, we die.

Upon a lily tremble
Two clear, round drops. They kiss,
Dissolve into one, and go rolling
Into the throat's abyss.

Calvin S. Brown

ADAMS OPFER

Die schönsten Früchte, frisch gepflückt,
Trägt er zum grünen Festaltar
Und bringt, mit Blumen reich geschmückt,
Sie fromm als Morgenopfer dar.

Erst blickt er froh, dann wird er still:
– O Herr, wie arm erschein' ich mir!
Wenn ich den Dank dir bringen will,
So borge ich selbst den von dir! –

ADAM'S OFFERING

The sweetest fruits, all freshly picked,
Unto the altar does he bear
And as a morning offering, decked
With flowers, devoutly lays them there.

Joyous at first, then hushed anew:
"Oh Lord, how poor I seem to me!
When I would bring Thee thanks, so do
I borrow even that from Thee!"

Lyn Goetze Snyder

DER BAUM IN DER WÜSTE

Es steht ein Baum im Wüstensand,
Der einzige, der dort gedieh;
Die Sonne hat ihn fast verbrannt,
Der Regen tränkt den durst'gen nie.

In seiner falben Krone hängt
Gewürzig eine Frucht voll Saft,
Er hat sein Mark hineingedrängt,
Sein Leben, seine höchste Kraft.

Die Stunde, wo sie überschwer
Zu Boden fallen muß, ist nah;
Es zieht kein Wanderer daher,
Und für ihn selbst ist sie nicht da.

THE TREE IN THE DESERT

In desert wastes there stands a tree,
The only one that there could thrive;
The sun has almost burnt it up,
No raindrops help it keep alive.

Amidst its faded leaves there hangs
A spicy fruit, full ripe and fair,
A fruit the tree has spent its life
And all its highest art to bear.

The moment nears. The heavy fruit
Must fall, it cannot linger on.
No wanderer comes near the tree.
It only knows the fruit is gone.

Frances Stillman

SOMMERBILD

Ich sah des Sommers letzte Rose stehn,
Sie war, als ob sie bluten könne, rot;
Da sprach ich schauernd im Vorübergehn:
So weit im Leben ist zu nah am Tod!

Es regte sich kein Hauch am heißen Tag,
Nur leise strich ein weißer Schmetterling;
Doch ob auch kaum die Luft sein Flügelschlag
Bewegte, sie empfand es und verging.

SUMMER IMAGE

The summer's last surviving rose I saw,
So crimson-hued as if it blood could shed.
Then, passing by, I said in doleful awe,
"So far in life is near the end we dread."

No breath of air stirred on that sultry day,
No being moved but one white butterfly;
Yet, though the air scarce felt its wings' light sway,
The red rose trembled, and I saw it die.

Gerd Gillhoff

HERBSTBILD

Dies ist ein Herbsttag, wie ich keinen sah!
Die Luft ist still, als atmete man kaum,
Und dennoch fallen raschelnd, fern und nah,
Die schönsten Früchte ab von jedem Baum.

O stört sie nicht, die Feier der Natur!
Dies ist die Lese, die sie selber hält,
Denn heute löst sich von den Zweigen nur,
Was vor dem milden Strahl der Sonne fällt.

PICTURE OF AUTUMN

This autumn day – I have not seen its peer.
The air so calm that loath to breathe seems all,
And yet, from every tree, both far and near,
Through rustling leaves the choicest fruits do fall.

Oh let no one disturb this harvest feast
Which Nature all alone enacts this day.
The fruits that fall are from their branch released
By gentle nudging of the sun's mild ray.

Alexander Gode

Theodor Storm

DIE STADT

Am grauen Strand, am grauen Meer
Und seitab liegt die Stadt;
Der Nebel drückt die Dächer schwer,
Und durch die Stille braust das Meer
Eintönig um die Stadt.

Es rauscht kein Wald, es schlägt im Mai
Kein Vogel ohn' Unterlaß;
Die Wandergans mit hartem Schrei
Nur fliegt in Herbstesnacht vorbei,
Am Strande weht das Gras.

Doch hängt mein ganzes Herz an dir,
Du graue Stadt am Meer;
Der Jugend Zauber für und für
Ruht lächelnd doch auf dir, auf dir,
Du graue Stadt am Meer.

THE TOWN

Gray is the sea; the shore is gray.
Behind it lies the town.
On roofs and sheds fog rests its spray.
Monotonously roars the bay
Around a quiet town.

No forest murmurs, and no sigh
Of birds is heard in May.
Wild geese in autumn nights fly by
And shriek their shrill, harsh, moaning cry.
Dry reeds in sand dunes play.

And yet, my heart belongs to you,
Gray city by the sea.
Enchantments of my youth endue
Forever smilingly just you,
Gray city by the sea.

                                        R. N. Linn

JULI

Klingt im Wind ein Wiegenlied,
Sonne warm herniedersieht,
Seine Ähren senkt das Korn,
Rote Beere schwillt am Dorn,
Schwer von Segen ist die Flur –
Junge Frau, was sinnst du nur?

JULY

In the breeze a humming tune
Warming rays from sun at noon
Swaying rye field, ears bent low
Bursting berries in the sloe
Countryside with blessings fraught
What, young woman, fills your thought?

Alexander Gode

Gottfried Keller

SIEHST DU DEN STERN

Siehst du den Stern im fernsten Blau,
Der flimmernd fast erbleicht?
Sein Licht braucht eine Ewigkeit,
Bis es dein Aug erreicht!

Vielleicht vor tausend Jahren schon
Zu Asche stob der Stern;
Und doch steht dort sein milder Schein
Noch immer still und fern.

Dem Wesen solchen Scheines gleicht,
Der ist und doch nicht ist,
O Lieb, dein anmutvolles Sein,
Wenn du gestorben bist!

SEE THERE THE STAR

See there the star. In distant blue
Its twinkle almost dies.
Its light took an eternity
Until it reached your eyes.

A thousand years ago perhaps
In ashes fell that star,
And yet, up there its gentle light
Keeps shining still and far.

Quite like that star, quite like its light
Which shines because it shone,
O love, I sense thy cherished warmth
Since thou art dead and gone.

Alexander Gode

ABENDLIED

Augen, meine lieben Fensterlein,
Gebt mir schon so lange holden Schein,
Lasset freundlich Bild um Bild herein:
Einmal werdet ihr verdunkelt sein!

Fallen einst die müden Lider zu,
Löscht ihr aus, dann hat die Seele Ruh;
Tastend streift sie ab die Wanderschuh,
Legt sich auch in ihre finstre Truh.

Noch zwei Fünklein sieht sie glimmend stehn,
Wie zwei Sternlein, innerlich zu sehn,
Bis sie schwanken, und dann auch vergehn,
Wie von eines Falters Flügelwehn.

Doch noch wandl ich auf dem Abendfeld,
Nur dem sinkenden Gestirn gesellt;
Trinkt, o Augen, was die Wimper hält,
Von dem goldnen Überfluß der Welt.

EVENING SONG

Eyes, ye treasured windows of my sight,
Have so long allowed me precious light;
Letting hosts of images delight,
Ere the fall of nature's darkening night.

When some day your weary lids must close,
Light fades out, the soul can find repose;
Gropingly her shoes aside she throws,
Lays her in her coffin so morose.

Yet two sparks she sees aglow on high,
Like two stars that charm the inner eye,
Till they flicker, and they too must die,
Wafted off on wings of butterfly.

Still I linger on the evening weald,
With the sinking sun to share the field,
Drink, O eyes, all that the lashes shield
Of the golden wealth the world doth yield.

                                        D. G. Wright

IN DER STADT

Wo sich drei Gassen kreuzen, krumm und enge,
Drei Züge wallen plötzlich sich entgegen
Und schlingen sich, gehemmt auf ihren Wegen,
Zu einem Knäul und lärmendem Gedränge.

Die Wachtparad mit gellen Trommelschlägen,
Ein Brautzug kommt mit Geigen und Gepränge,
Ein Leichenzug klagt seine Grabgesänge:
Das alles stockt, es kann kein Glied sich regen.

Verstummt sind Geiger, Pfaff und Trommelschläger;
Der dicke Hauptmann flucht, daß niemand weiche,
Gelächter schallet aus dem Freudenzug.

Doch oben, auf den Schultern schwarzer Träger
Starrt in der Mitte kalt und still die Leiche
Mit blinden Augen in den Wolkenflug.

IN THE CITY

Where intersect three narrow, crooked lanes,
Three separate groups emerge and headlong meet.
Unable to move forward or retreat,
They tangle closely as in raveled skeins.

The watch, parading to the drums' brisk beat,
A wedding gay, with fiddlers in its train,
A funeral crowd, intoning mournful strains,
Move to a halt till stock-still rest all feet.

Now fiddlers, priest, and drummers silent fall,
The red-faced, stoutish captain curses all,
The members of the party laugh aloud.

But in the middle black-garbed bearers hold
Aloft the corpse, which, motionless and cold,
Stares up, unseeing, at a drifting cloud.

Gerd Gillhoff

DER SCHULGENOSS

Wohin hat dich dein guter Stern gezogen,
O Schulgenoß aus ersten Knabenjahren?
Wie weit sind auseinander wir gefahren
In unsern Schifflein auf des Lebens Wogen!

Wenn wir die Untersten der Klasse waren,
Wie haben wir treuherzig uns betrogen,
Erfinderisch und schwärmrisch uns belogen
Von Aventüren, Liebschaft und Gefahren!

Da seh ich just, beim Schimmer der Laterne,
Wie mir gebückt, zerlumpt ein Vagabund
Mit einem Häscher scheu vorübergeht—!

So also wendeten sich unsre Sterne?
Und so hat es gewuchert, unser Pfund?
Du bist ein Schelm geworden—ich Poet!

THE SCHOOL COMPANION

O whither were you by your good fate guided,
Companion of my early boyhood days?
How far we drifted from each other's gaze,
As o'er the sea of life our frail barks glided!

In school we never won the master's praise,
But each to each effusively confided
Ingenious tales wherein ourselves we prided
On grand amours, adventures, and affrays.

This very moment, in a street lamp's light,
I see a bowed and ragged vagabond,
Beside a constable, slink shyly by.

Was this the course our stars traced in their flight?
Was it to this account we turned our pound?
A knave have you become—a poet I!

Gerd Gillhoff

Conrad Ferdinand Meyer

JETZT REDE DU

Du warest mir ein täglich Wanderziel,
Viellieber Wald, in dumpfen Jugendtagen,
Ich hatte dir geträumten Glücks so viel
Anzuvertraun, so wahren Schmerz zu klagen.

Und wieder such ich dich, du dunkler Hort,
Und deines Wipfelmeers gewaltig Rauschen –
Jetzt rede du ! Ich lasse dir das Wort !
Verstummt ist Klag und Jubel. Ich will lauschen.

NOW YOU SHALL SPEAK

Once you were daily pilgrimage to me,
Beloved wood, when I was young and sad,
And told you all my dreams of happiness
And all the real troubles that I had.

Now once again I seek your dim retreat
Where winds, like tides in treetops, rush and darken.
Now you shall speak! I leave the words to you!
Stilled are my joys and troubles. I shall hearken.

Frances Stillman

DER RÖMISCHE BRUNNEN

Aufsteigt der Strahl und fallend gießt
Er voll der Marmorschale Rund,
Die, sich verschleiernd, überfließt
In einer zweiten Schale Grund;
Die zweite gibt, sie wird zu reich,
Der dritten wallend ihre Flut,
Und jede nimmt und gibt zugleich
Und strömt und ruht.

THE ROMAN FOUNTAIN

Up shoots the stream and falling pours
Its flood into the marble urn,
Which, veiled in lacey froth, outpours
Into a lower bowl in turn;
To still a third its surplus store
The second gives and rolling grows;
Each gives and takes forevermore
And rests and flows. . .

Isabel S. MacInnes

FÜLLE

Genug ist nicht genug! Gepriesen werde
Der Herbst! Kein Ast, der seiner Frucht entbehrte!
Tief beugt sich mancher allzureich beschwerte,
Der Apfel fällt mit dumpfem Laut zur Erde.

Genug ist nicht genug! Es lacht im Laube!
Die saftige Pfirsche winkt dem durstigen Munde!
Die trunknen Wespen summen in die Runde:
,,Genug ist nicht genug!" um eine Traube.

Genug ist nicht genug! Mit vollen Zügen
Schlürft Dichtergeist am Borne des Genusses,
Das Herz, auch es bedarf des Überflusses,
Genug kann nie und nimmermehr genügen!

ABUNDANCE

Enough is not enough! Glory to Autumn!
No bough but bears its harvest, ripe and sound.
Some, overladen, bend beneath their burden.
An apple softly thuds upon the ground.

Enough is not enough! Laughter in copses.
The juicy peach beckons the thirsty tongue.
And drunken wasps cluster around the grapevine –
"Enough is not enough!" their buzzing song.

Enough is not enough! From all this plenty
Drink greedy gulps of joy to fire the brain.
The heart, too, needs its surfeit of abundance.
Enough can never be enough again.

Helen Sebba

ZWEI SEGEL

Zwei Segel erhellend
Die tiefblaue Bucht!
Zwei Segel sich schwellend
Zu ruhiger Flucht!

Wie eins in den Winden
Sich wölbt und bewegt,
Wird auch das Empfinden
Des andern erregt.

Begehrt eins zu hasten,
Das andre geht schnell,
Verlangt eins zu rasten,
Ruht auch sein Gesell.

TWO SAILS

Two sails make bright
The dark-blue bay;
Two sails stretch tight
To heave away.

When wind pours through,
One grows immense;
The other one, too,
Responds and is tense.

When one makes a run
Locked is their gait;
When calm strikes the one,
The other will wait.

Kurt J. Fickert

DER GESANG DES MEERES

Wolken, meine Kinder, wandern gehen
Wollt ihr? Fahret wohl! Auf Wiedersehen!
Eure wandellustigen Gestalten
Kann ich nicht in Mutterbanden halten.

Ihr langweilet euch auf meinen Wogen,
Dort die Erde hat euch angezogen:
Küsten, Klippen und des Leuchtturms Feuer!
Ziehet, Kinder! Geht auf Abenteuer!

Segelt, kühne Schiffer, in den Lüften!
Such die Gipfel! Ruhet über Klüften!
Brauet Stürme! Blitzet! Liefert Schlachten!
Traget glüh'nden Kampfes Purpurtrachten!

Rauscht im Regen! Murmelt in den Quellen!
Füllt die Brunnen! Rieselt in die Wellen!
Braust in Strömen durch die Lande nieder –
Kommet, meine Kinder, kommet wieder!

THE SONG OF THE SEA

Oh clouds, my children, is your will to roam?
Then go! Farewell, until you come back home!
I can no more your restless shapes retain
Within the bonds of my maternal rein

Now you are weary of my waves, I see,
The land has lured you there away from me:
The shores, the cliffs, the beacon's fiery glow!
Be off, and seek adventure, children, go!

Float, fearless sailors, gently through the air!
Seek hill-tops, and ravines, and linger there!
Engender storms, and strike with blinding light!
And don the purple garb of ardent fight!

Rush in the rain! Murmur in springs below!
Refresh the wells! Ripple in ebb and flow!
Stream down in torrents gushing through the plain,
And come, my children, back to me again!

D. G. Wright

CHOR DER TOTEN

Wir Toten, wir Toten sind größere Heere
Als ihr auf der Erde, als ihr auf dem Meere!
Wir pflügten das Feld mit geduldigen Taten,
Ihr schwinget die Sichel und schneidet die Saaten,
Und was wir vollendet und was wir begonnen,
Das füllt noch dort oben die rauschenden Bronnen,
Und all unser Lieben und Hassen und Hadern,
Das klopft noch dort oben in sterblichen Adern,
Und was wir an gültigen Sätzen gefunden,
Dran bleibt aller irdische Wandel gebunden,
Und unsere Töne, Gebilde, Gedichte
Erkämpfen den Lorbeer im strahlenden Lichte,
Wir suchen noch immer die menschlichen Ziele –
Drum ehret und opfert! Denn unser sind viele!

THE CHORUS OF THE DEAD

We dead men, we dead men can muster more legions
Than all of you mortals in all the world's regions!
Where we ploughed the fields for the deeds we were sowing
There now sinks the harvest your sickles are mowing,
And what we completed or merely decided
Up there keeps your fountains with water provided,
And all our loving and hating and yearning,
Up there warms your blood and you still feel it burning,
By laws and by measures which we once erected
Still all that you do in your world is directed,
And what we in stone, sound, or word once created
Is crowned in the light by the world it elated.
We still are pursuing the goals of the living.
Revere our numbers. We still are the giving.

Meno Spann

AM HIMMELSTOR

Mir träumt, ich komm ans Himmelstor
Und finde dich, die Süße!
Du saßest bei dem Quell davor
Und wuschest dir die Füße.

Du wuschest, wuschest ohne Rast
Den blendend weißen Schimmer,
Begannst mit wunderlicher Hast
Dein Werk von neuem immer.

Ich frug: „Was badest du dich hier
Mit tränennassen Wangen?"
Du sprachst: „Weil ich im Staub mit dir,
So tief im Staub gegangen."

AT THE GATE OF HEAVEN

I dreamt I came to heaven's gate,
And found you there, my sweet!
Beside the fountain you did wait,
And bathe your dainty feet.

You washed the shimmer dazzling white,
You washed with might and main,
Then hastily, a curious sight,
Began all o'er again.

I asked: What makes you bathe your feet?
Your eyes, what makes them weep?"
"I walked," you said, "with you a street
On which the dust lay deep."

D. G. Wright

Ferdinand von Saar

AUF EINEN ALTEN SCHLOSSPARK

Nie hat die Lust als Ariadnefaden
Sich durch dies grüne Labyrinth gezogen;
Man glättete hier stets des Lebens Wogen
Zum Teich Bethesda, um sich rein zu baden.

Eremitagen, Grotten an den Pfaden
Für schöne Seelen, die sich selbst belogen,
Als sie sich nannten von der Welt betrogen,
Und brünstig sah'n nach himmlischen Gestaden.

Hier stand die Zeit still, die, vom blut'gen Ruhme
Des Korsen kaum befreit, demütig wieder
Zu Füßen sank dem alten Heiligtume.

Hier weh'n noch Matthissons schwermüt'ge Lieder,
Hier blüht und duftet noch die blaue Blume,
Und wandelt Stillings Geist noch auf und nieder.

ON AN OLD CASTLE-PARK

Desire has never, through this maze's green,
Charted its way like Ariadne's thread;
Here life's waves were always smoothed and led
Into Bethesda's pond, to bathe men clean.

Grottoes and arbors lined this serpentine
For lofty spirits, who each time they said
The world had tricked them, tricked themselves instead,
Dreaming in pious lust of heaven's demesne.

Here time, which from Napoleon's bloody fame
Had scarcely been set free, stood still to pay
Its humble homage at the old god's flame.

Here hang the notes of Matthisson's sad lay,
Here the blue flower's perfume clings the same,
And here the ghost of Stilling goes its way.

George C. Schoolfield

Martin Greif

VOR DER ERNTE

Nun störet die Ähren im Felde
Ein leiser Hauch,
Wenn eine sich beugt, so bebet
Die andre auch.

Es ist, als ahnten sie alle
Der Sichel Schnitt –
Die Blumen und fremden Halme
Erzittern mit.

BEFORE THE HARVEST

Now all of the grain stalks stir
To a whispered breeze;
When two of them tremble, the others
Tremble with these.

They seem to be sensing the ruin
The scythe will strew;
The flowers and grainless grasses
Are trembling too.

Clark Stillman

Christian Wagner

SYRINGEN

Fast überirdisch dünkt mich euer Grüßen,
Syringen ihr, mit eurem Duft, dem süßen!

Wohl darf ich euch nach Geisterweise werten:
Ein schwellend Duftlied seid ihr von Verklärten.

Gott, wie ich doch in dieser blauen Kühle
Der Blumenwolke hier mich wohlig fühle!

Süß heimlich ahnend, was hineinverwoben,
Wie fühl ich mich so frei, so stolz gehoben!

Bin ich es selbst, des einstig Erdenwesen
Nun auch einmal zu solchem Glanz genesen?

Sinds meine Lieben, die, ach, längst begraben,
In diesen Düften Fühlung mit mir haben?

LILACS

As if from heaven so you now me greet
You lilac blossoms with your scent so sweet.

In spirit-like demeanor I evoke you best:
A swelling, fragrant song of souls at rest.

God, how since coming to this coolness blue
Of blooming cloud, I tranquil, happy grew.

In secret, sweetly sensing how 't was spun,
I feel exalted, lifted to the sun.

Is it myself who once to earth was bound
And now in splendor his reward has found?

Are they my loved ones who, long in their graves,
Communicate with me through fragrant waves?

Dorothea M. Singer

Eugen Höfling

O ALTE BURSCHENHERRLICHKEIT

O alte Burschenherrlichkeit!
Wohin bist du verschwunden?
Nie kehrst du wieder, goldne Zeit,
So froh und ungebunden!
Vergebens spähe ich umher,
Ich finde deine Spur nicht mehr.
    O jerum, jerum, jerum!
    O quae mutatio rerum!

Drum, Freunde, reichet euch die Hand,
Damit es sich erneue,
Der alten Freundschaft heiliges Band,
Das alte Band der Treue.
Klingt an und hebt die Gläser hoch,
Die alten Burschen leben noch,
    Noch lebt die alte Treue!
    Noch lebt die alte Treue!

OLD STUDENT DAYS

O glory of old student ways,
Wherever have you vanished?
You'll ne'er return, O golden days,
Your gaiety is banished.
I look around, alas, in vain,
I find no trace of you again.
         O jerum, jerum, jerum!
         O quae mutatio rerum!

So, friends, join hands and gather round,
Let us remember ever.
The song of friendship let resound,
This bond we'll never sever.
So clink and raise your glasses high,
May friends and friendship never die!
         Let us remember ever!
         Let us remember ever!

Francis Owen

Detlev von Liliencron

DIE MUSIK KOMMT

Klingling, bumbum und tschingdada,
Zieht im Triumph der Perserschah?
Und um die Ecke brausend brichts
Wie Tubaton des Weltgerichts,
Voran der Schellenträger.

Brumbrum, das große Bombardon,
Der Beckenschlag, das Helikon,
Die Pikkolo, der Zinkenist,
Die Türkentrommel, der Flötist,
Und dann der Herre Hauptmann.

Der Hauptmann naht mit stolzem Sinn,
Die Schuppenketten unterm Kinn,
Die Schärpe schnürt den schlanken Leib,
Beim Zeus! das ist kein Zeitvertreib;
Und dann die Herren Leutnants.

Zwei Leutnants, rosenrot und braun,
Die Fahne schützen sie als Zaun,
Die Fahne kommt, den Hut nimm ab,
Der bleiben treu wir bis ins Grab!
Und dann die Grenadiere.

Der Grenadier im strammen Tritt,
In Schritt und Tritt und Tritt und Schritt,
Das stampft und dröhnt und klappt und flirrt,
Laternenglas und Fenster klirrt;
Und dann die kleinen Mädchen.

THE BAND MARCHES

Klingling, boomboom, and chingdada –
A triumph of the Persian Shah?
It rounds the corner with a boom
Like trumpets of the Day of Doom,
In front the big drum major.

Broombroom, the monster bombardon,
The cymbals and the helicon,
The cornet and the piccolo,
The big bass drum, the flute also,
And then the lord high captain.

The haughty captain comes in sight.
His helmet strap is neat and tight;
A tight sash gives a martial air –
By Jove, this is no light affair!
And then the fine lieutenants.

The two lieutenants, red and tan,
Surround the flag, a wall of man!
The flag arrives: take off your hat –
We will be true till death to that!
And then the common privates.

The privates march with martial step,
With hep! and step, and step and hep!
They stamp and rumble, clatter, shake,
Till window panes and streetlights quake –
And then the little schoolgirls.

Die Mädchen alle, Kopf an Kopf,
Das Auge blau und blond der Zopf,
Aus Tür und Tor und Hof und Haus
Schaut Mine, Trine, Stine aus;
Vorbei ist die Musike.

Klingling, tschingtsching und Paukenkrach,
Noch aus der Ferne tönt es schwach,
Ganz leise bumbum bumbum tsching;
Zog da ein bunter Schmetterling,
Tschingtsching, bum, um die Ecke?

The little girls, head after head –
From door and gate and yard and shed,
With eyes of blue and pigtailed hair,
How Betty, Hetty, Letty stare.
The music has departed.

Klingling, chingching, and kettledrums,
Faint from the distance still it comes,
Quite softly, boomboomboomboom ching –
Did a bright butterfly take wing,
Chingching, boom, round the corner?

Calvin S. Brown

INDEX OF
TITLES AND BEGINNINGS OF GERMAN POEMS

Abend (*Gryphius*)   14
Abendlied (*Claudius*)   48
Abendlied (*Keller*)   228
Abendphantasie (*Hölderlin*)   122
Abendständchen (*Brentano*)   136
Ach, um deine feuchten Schwingen (*Goethe*)   70
Adams Opfer (*Hebbel*)   214
Als der erste Schnee fiel (*Goeckingk*)   56
Am Brunnen vor dem Tore (*Müller*)   160
Am grauen Strand (*Storm*)   222
Am Himmelstor (*Meyer*)   246
An den Mond (*Goethe*)   66
An die Entfernte (*Lenau*)   182
An die Parzen (*Hölderlin*)   126
An sich (*Fleming*)   12
An sie umb einen Kuß (*Haugwitz*)   28
Auch das Schöne muß sterben (*Schiller*)   116
Auf dem Teich, dem regungslosen (*Lenau*)   186
Auf den Tod eines Kindes (*Uhland*)   144
Auf eine holländische Landschaft (*Lenau*)   184
Auf einen alten Schloßpark (*Saar*)   248
Auf ihrem Leibrößlein (*Mörike*)   198
Aufsteigt der Strahl (*Meyer*)   236
Augen, meine lieben Fensterlein (*Keller*)   228
Bin ich nüchtern (*Goeckingk*)   58
Bitte (*Lenau*)   192
Chor der Toten (*Meyer*)   244
Das Glück (*Schiller*)   106
Das Ideal und das Leben (*Schiller*)   112
Das Veilchen (*Goethe*)   62

Das verlassene Mägdlein (*Mörike*) — 200

Das Wandern ist des Müllers Lust (*Müller*) — 158

Denk es, o Seele (*Mörike*) — 206

Der Baum in der Wüste (*Hebbel*) — 216

Der Einsiedler (*Eichendorff*) — 148

Der frohe Wandersmann (*Eichendorff*) — 146

Der Gärtner (*Mörike*) — 198

Der Gesang des Meeres (*Meyer*) — 242

Der Glantz, der Blitz (*Haugwitz*) — 28

Der Lindenbaum (*Müller*) — 160

Der Mond ist aufgegangen (*Claudius*) — 48

Der römische Brunnen (*Meyer*) — 236

Der schnelle Tag ist hin (*Gryphius*) — 14

Der Schulgenoß (*Keller*) — 232

Der Spinnerin Lied (*Brentano*) — 138

Der Tod (*Hölderlin*) — 130

Der Tod und das Mädchen (*Claudius*) — 42

Des Knaben Berglied (*Uhland*) — 140

Des Menschen Seele gleicht dem Wasser (*Goethe*) — 78

Die Drei (*Lenau*) — 190

Die drei Zigeuner (*Lenau*) — 188

Die frühen Gräber (*Klopstock*) — 54

Die linden Lüfte sind erwacht (*Uhland*) — 142

Die Musik kommt (*Liliencron*) — 256

Die Mutter bei der Wiege (*Claudius*) — 56

Die Nachtblume (*Eichendorff*) — 152

Die Rose, die Lilie, die Taube, die Sonne (*Heine*) — 174

Die schönsten Früchte (*Hebbel*) — 214

Die Stadt (*Storm*) — 222

Die Sternseherin Lise (*Claudius*) — 46

Die Wanderratten (*Heine*) — 168

Die Zukunft decket (*Goethe*) — 96

Dies ist ein Herbsttag (*Hebbel*) — 220

Diese Rose pflück ich hier (*Lenau*)   182

Drei Reiter nach verlorner Schlacht (*Lenau*)   190

Drei Zigeuner fand ich einmal (*Lenau*)   188

Du bist min (*Unbekannter Dichter*)   4

Du kamst, du gingst (*Uhland*)   144

Du siehst, wohin du siehst (*Gryphius*)   16

Du warest mir ein täglich Wanderziel (*Meyer*)   234

Ein Fichtenbaum steht einsam (*Heine*)   166

Ein Pfeil geht zwar geschwind (*Hunold*)   30

Ein Tännlein grünet wo (*Mörike*)   206

Ein Traum, ein Traum ist unser Leben (*Herder*)   52

Ein Veilchen auf der Wiese stand (*Goethe*)   62

Eitelkeit der Welt (*Gryphius*)   16

Endlich bleibt nicht ewig aus (*Günther*)   32

Er erschreckt uns (*Hölderlin*)   130

Es ist schon spät (*Eichendorff*)   154

Es fürchte die Götter (*Goethe*)   82

Es gibt zwei Sorten Ratten (*Heine*)   168

Es sang vor langen Jahren (*Brentano*)   138

Es steht ein Baum (*Hebbel*)   216

Es war, als hätt der Himmel (*Eichendorff*)   150

Es war ein alter König (*Heine*)   164

Es wird der bleiche Tod (*Hoffmannswaldau*)   26

Euch bedaur ich, unglückselige Sterne (*Goethe*)   72

Ewigklar und spiegelrein (*Schiller*)   112

Frühlingsglaube (*Uhland*)   142

Früh, wann die Hähne krähn (*Mörike*)   200

Fülle (*Meyer*)   238

Füllest wieder (*Goethe*)   66

Fast überirdisch (*Wagner*)   252

Geh aus, mein Herz (*Gerhardt*)   8

Gelassen stieg die Nacht (*Mörike*)   202

Genug ist nicht genug (*Meyer*)   238

Gesang der Geister über den Wassern (*Goethe*) 78

Gleich einem König (*Goeckingk*) 56

Hälfte des Lebens (*Hölderlin*) 128

Harfenspieler (*Goethe*) 76

Heidenröslein (*Goethe*) 64

Herbstbild (*Hebbel*) 220

Hör, es klagt die Flöte wieder (*Brentano*) 136

Hyperions Schicksalslied (*Hölderlin*) 124

Ich bin vom Berg der Hirtenknab (*Uhland*) 140

Ich hab die Nacht geträumet (*Unbekannter Dichter*) 132

Ich hatte einst ein schönes Vaterland (*Heine*) 178

Ich sah des Sommers letzte Rose stehn (*Hebbel*) 218

Ich sehe oft um Mitternacht (*Claudius*) 46

Ich und du (*Hebbel*) 212

Ich war erst sechzehn Sommer alt (*Claudius*) 38

Ich zôch mir einen Valken (*Der von Kürenberg*) 2

Ihr naht euch wieder, schwankende Gestalten (*Goethe*) 90

Ihr wandelt droben im Licht (*Hölderlin*) 124

In der Stadt (*Keller*) 230

Ist nicht heilig mein Herz (*Hölderlin*) 118

Jetzt rede du (*Meyer*) 234

Juli (*Storm*) 224

Kind! Dreimal süßes Kind (*Gryphius*) 22

Klingling, Bumbum (*Liliencron*) 256

Klingt im Wind ein Wiegenlied (*Storm*) 224

Komm, Trost der Welt (*Eichendorff*) 148

Kriegslied (*Claudius*) 44

Laß, o Welt (*Mörike*) 204

Leise zieht durch mein Gemüt (*Heine*) 162

Lied der Parzen (*Goethe*) 82

Lynkeus der Türmer (*Goethe*) 88

Mainacht (*Hölty*) 54

Menschenbeifall (*Hölderlin*) 118

264

Menschliches Elende (*Gryphius*) 18
Mir träumt, ich komm ans Himmelstor (*Meyer*) 246
Mit gelben Birnen hänget (*Hölderlin*) 128
Mondnacht (*Eichendorff*) 150
Morgenrot (*Hauff*) 180
Müde schleichen hier die Bäche (*Lenau*) 184
Nach dem ersten nächtlichen Besuche (*Goeckingk*) 58
Nacht ist wie ein stilles Meer (*Eichendorff*) 152
Nachtgedanken (*Goethe*) 72
Nänie (*Schiller*) 116
Natur und Kunst (*Goethe*) 86
Nie hat die Lust (*Saar*) 248
Nun störet die Ähren im Felde (*Greif*) 250
Nur einen Sommer gönnt (*Hölderlin*) 126
O alte Burschenherrlichkeit (*Höfling*) 254
O lieb, so lang du lieben kannst (*Freiligrath*) 208
Owê war sint verswunden (*Walther von der Vogelweide*) 6
Phidile (*Claudius*) 38
Reiters Morgengesang (*Hauff*) 180
Sah ein Knab' ein Röslein stehn (*Goethe*) 64
Schilflied (V) (*Lenau*) 186
Schlaf, süßer Knabe (*Claudius*) 36
Schläft ein Lied (*Eichendorff*) 156
Schön-Rohtraut (*Mörike*) 194
Sei dennoch unverzagt (*Fleming*) 12
Selig, welchen die Götter (*Schiller*) 106
Siehst du den Stern (*Keller*) 226
Singet leise (*Brentano*) 134
'S ist Krieg (*Claudius*) 44
Sokrates und Alkibiades (*Hölderlin*) 120
Sommerbild (*Hebbel*) 218
Sprüche (*Goethe*) 98
Symbolum (*Goethe*) 96

INDEX OF GERMAN POEMS

Syringen (*Wagner*) 252
Tränen des Vaterlandes (*Gryphius*) 20
Trostaria (*Günther*) 32
Über die Geburt Christi (*Gryphius*) 22
Über die Zeit (*Hunold*) 30
Um Mitternacht (*Goethe*) 74
Um Mitternacht (*Mörike*) 202
Um Mitternacht ging ich (*Goethe*) 74
Urworte, Orphisch (*Goethe*) 92
Verborgenheit (*Mörike*) 204
Vergänglichkeit der Schönheit (*Hoffmannswaldau*) 26
Vor der Ernte (*Greif*) 250
Vor seiner Hütte (*Hölderlin*) 122
Vorüber! Ach vorüber (*Claudius*) 42
Waldgespräch (*Eichendorff*) 154
Wanderschaft (*Müller*) 158
Warum huldigest du (*Hölderlin*) 120
Was sind wir menschen doch (*Gryphius*) 18
Wem Gott will rechte Gunst erweisen (*Eichendorff*) 146
Weil auf mir, du dunkles Auge (*Lenau*) 192
Wenn der silberne Mond (*Hölty*) 54
Wer nie sein Brot mit Tränen aß (*Goethe*) 76
Wie an dem Tag (*Goethe*) 92
Wie heißt König Ringangs Töchterlein (*Mörike*) 194
Wiegenlied (*Brentano*) 134
Willkommen, o silberner Mond (*Klopstock*) 34
Wir sind doch nunmehr ganz (*Gryphius*) 20
Wir träumten voneinander (*Hebbel*) 212
Wir Toten, wir Toten (*Meyer*) 244
Wo? (*Heine*) 176
Wohin hat dich (*Keller*) 232
Wolken, meine Kinder (*Meyer*) 242
Wo sich drei Gassen kreuzen (*Keller*) 230

Wo sind die Stunden (*Hoffmannswaldau*)   24

Wo wird einst des Wandermüden (*Heine*)   176

Wünschelrute (*Eichendorff*)   156

Zum Sehen geboren (*Goethe*)   88

Zwei Segel (*Meyer*)   240

Zwei Segel erhellend (*Meyer*)   240

Zueignung (*Goethe*)   90

INDEX OF TRANSLATORS

Benedict, Stewart H.   147
Bloch, Albert   45
Brown, Calvin S.   213, 259
Brown, Oliver   145
Brown, W. Edward   123
Buehne, Sheema Z.   47, 203
Fickert, Kurt J.   241
Friedman, Philip Allan   125
Gillhoff, Gerd   75, 91, 155, 189, 191, 201, 219, 231, 233
Gode, Alexander   3, 5, 25, 35, 41, 51, 53, 63, 69, 73, 89, 97, 105,
                      111, 117, 127, 129, 139, 179, 183, 221, 225, 227
Hamburger, Michael   87
Hilty, Palmer   121
Issawi, Charles   173, 175, 211
Jennings, Anne   135, 137
Kahn, R. L.   81
Knight, Max, and Fabry, Joseph   95
Linn, R. N.   223
Livermore, Janet Alison   7
MacInnes, Isabel S.   153, 197, 237
Marvin, Lynda A.   65
Norden, Heinz   101
Norton, Roger C.   185, 187
Owen, Francis   141, 159, 161, 163, 181, 255
Passage, Charles E.   85, 207
Richter, Margaret R.   167
Rose, Ernst   199
Salinger, Herman   77
Schoolfield, George C.   11, 13, 15, 17, 19, 21, 23, 27, 29,
                                        31, 33, 57, 61, 193, 249
Scott, Aurelia G.   71

INDEX OF TRANSLATORS

Sebba, Helen	55, 177, 239
Singer, Dorothea M.	43, 253
Snyder, Lyn Goetze	131, 215
Spann, Meno	149, 245
Stillman, Clark	251
Stillman, Frances	217, 235
Trask, Willard R., and Gode, Alexander	129
Turner, Alison	157
Weimar, Karl	165
Winston, Richard	115
Wright, D. G.	37, 133, 151, 205, 229, 243, 247
Zwart, Martin	119, 143